Teaching Mixed Media to Children

Teaching Mixed Media to Children

Written by
Karla Cikánová

CRAFTSMAN HOUSE

Designed and produced by Aventinum Publishing House,
Prague, Czech Republic

This edition first published in 1995 by Craftsman House BVI Ltd.
Distributed in Australia by Craftsman House,
20 Barcoo Street,
East Roseville, NSW 2069, Australia

Distributed internationally through the following offices:

USA
STBS Ltd.
PO Box 786
Cooper Station
New York
NY 10276

EUROPE
G+B Arts International (Europe) Ltd.
St Johanns-Vorstadt 19
Postfach
4004 Basel
Switzerland

ASIA
STBS (Singapore) Pte Ltd.
No. 25 Tannery Road
Singapore 1334
Republic of Singapore

ISBN 976 6410 04 6

Written by Karla Cikánová
Translated by Elizabeth Novak

Instructive drawings by Karla Cikánová
Photographs by Karla Cikánová, Radek Melka, Jan Pohribný, Vladimír Rocman,
and Stanislav Vaněk
Graphic design by Daruše Singerová

Printed in the Czech Republic
1/99/47/51−01

Contents

Preface   7

1
Stroking the Surface, Discovering Shape   11

From flat paper to spatial shape. How much can paper stand? Can space
be bad-tempered? Touching games. What else can we use for modelling?

2
Contact with Nature   33

Contact with trees. Paper beetles. Were there dragons in prehistoric times?
Playing at prehistoric cave artists. Oh to be a bird for just a little while!
Interesting tetrapods. Animal masks.

3
How Nature Modelled Us   57

Plasticine figures with movable limbs. We examine our own hands. Leafing through
our own head? Different masks. Helmets and hats not only change the shape
of our head. Hoods and overalls – empaquetage (wrapping up) of the human body.

4
Ordinary Things?   81

The transformation of things. No chair is the same. Assemblage – the strange
meeting of objects. Pencils for a giant. Clocks to show spring. Children
as designers. Cars, aeroplanes and other flying objects. Toys for the first-year
pupils. Some still lifes with alarm clocks.

5
People's Homes   105

Building does not only mean putting one brick next to another, a house next
to a house. You find the material and you build a house. Tents and other types
of shelter. Constructions rising from the surface of one sheet of paper.
Climbing frames and slides. Towers.

Preface

What the children said about shape:

'Best of all round shapes I like my ball and then strawberry dumplings' … 'The cleverest of all round shapes is the head of a grown-up' … 'The most wonderful shapes are tiny little seeds, one of them remembers that it should become a fir tree, and the other that maybe it will be an apple tree' … 'I love best of all to stroke water and a kitten' … 'When I am scared I am like a prickly ball, like a hedgehog or a cactus'… 'A house is like a huge beautiful or ugly coat for many people' … 'People have sewn trousers to fit them, but chairs, too' … 'A spire points to where people have not got to know it yet' … 'Many statues are hidden in the sculptor's clay' … 'Michelangelo cut the angry David out of stone, but he did not manage Goliath any more' … 'The sculptor carries his statues about with him in his head.'

The very first thing children grip in their hands is probably their mother's index finger or thumb. It is only then that babies begin – carefully and step by step – to investigate their closest surroundings with all their senses, touch playing the most important part. The world is full of shapes and it is a difficult job requiring repeated experiments to differentiate between large and small, round and angular, soft and hard. Babies discover what is pleasant, enjoy the softness or the mystery of surfaces, learn to grasp things in the best and safest possible manner and have such a good look at the shape that they know immediately what they are dealing with. This is what all generations have done and will continue to do.

The present generation of 10-year-olds, and even younger children, however, manage unusually quickly to handle push buttons and keys of computer games or mechanical toys and later computers themselves. They touch the push buttons with their index fingers only and suddenly we wonder what has happened to their sense of touch, so important for the development of human beings and their recognition of the world. Is it perhaps pushed into the background by other, more recently acquired skills?

I realise that nowadays children get to know the material world largely through television. They learn about animate and inanimate nature, animals, plants and all sorts of objects without being able to reach for them, weigh them in their hands, stroke them, establish lasting contact with them and classify them as part of their experience. Thanks to television a child can observe within a short period of time how an astronaut behaves in space, whether a volcano is still erupting or what damage an earthquake has caused, how chickens hatch and what fishermen have caught in their nets. It seems that the impoverishment of the sense of touch (direct contact with shapes) is the price paid by the present generation for their use of electronics. Their sense of observation is flooded with unprecedented impressions and pictorial information offered by the television screen. Electronics is the work of the human brain, just as once upon a time was the discovery of the wheel and later the microscope or rocket fuel, and they affect all mankind. They are and will remain an extension of human thought.

Nevertheless, there is nothing to replace the sense of touch. Not only children, but adults also enjoy cuddling small animals. The sensation cannot be replaced by television images. It is part of our experience in life that it is quite different to go yourself to pick mushrooms, to fish in the pond or to catch a butterfly and have a good look at it. Children who are allowed to throw a clumsy little pot on a wheel with their own hands will discover much more than they would watching a film on ceramics. Children who have had the chance to look after or ride a live horse, will draw or model it quite differently.

Human beings only develop a fully-rounded personality if in childhood those traits that make them fit for this world are not neglected. That means a great measure of reason and feeling, fantasy and above all unbounded curiosity. Art education here plays a most important part. This is why we are offering you the third volume in the series of publications on creative activities designed for 8 to 12-year-olds. This volume is dedicated to spatial creativity, reminding us that creative activities – drawing, painting, collage, spatial creation – cannot be separated. The text is again addressed to adults dealing with the art education of children, that is teachers, educationalists and parents.

The publication introduces the children through play to shape – its surface, construction, placing in space. The first chapter develops children's spatial creative thought in direct contact with easily available materials. They try out various simple methods of using paper, plastic modelling clay, plasticine, string, small pieces of wood etc.

The following five chapters discuss suggestions for the expression of concrete shapes and structures of animate and inanimate nature. The illustrations offer various possibilities of approach and how to become familiar with the human figure. The children may choose to create paper toys or to model and animate various objects or design small houses, towers and castles.

The topics are based on children's natural need, individually and collectively, to discuss the observed shapes of animate and inanimate nature, but they also attempt in the form of play to create and change the world according to their own fantasies. We shall deal with the creation of fantastic animals, masks, the modelling of fantastic chairs, and so on.

The technical procedures for dealing with the various materials are given in the individual chapters. For inspiration and the search of creative interdependence, photographs of the natural and artifical world are given at the end of each chapter, and last but not least of the works of the artists.

All the art work of the 8 to 12-year-olds was produced, verified and documented under the guidance of the author, a teacher at a primary school in Prague.

Karla Cikánová

1

2

Stroking the Surface, Discovering Shape

From flat paper to spatial shape. How much can paper stand? Can space be bad-tempered? Touching games. What else can we use for modelling?

We were all born into the world of shapes and are not flat ourselves. We have three dimensions, height, width and depth. We know very well that even the thinnest leaf in a book, however much it insists that it is flat, misleads us. It just is not true. Even a sheet of paper has depth, though we prefer to call it thickness, strength. Nevertheless, we tend to forget this thickness and imagine that tailors manage to sew clothes from material that looks like a flat surface. First they make a pattern and then they stitch the various pieces of material together so that we can put them on. A shoemaker does the same when making our shoes. It is what children do when they fold a sheet of paper into a hat or when they put up a tent in the garden made from an ordinary blanket. In some of the photographs in this book you will see that from a sheet of paper you can make a humming bird, an owl or a tiger, an aeroplane, a car or a castle. Though we will also discuss other materials that children can use for modelling, first we will talk about paper, which is readily accessible.

Small children are easily excited when large sheets of newspaper are put in front of them. And what do they do with them? How can they get hold

1 *Coarse textile*, sackcloth is not pleasant to the touch. Just imagine if your shirt were made of it. The children were fascinated by coarse textiles, they played with them, pulled threads, enlarged artificial holes. Then they made up an interesting picture from the remnants in which the threads sometimes moved as if they were alive. Then they carefully covered the entire area with diluted colourless glue.

2 *It is easy to make fans from folded paper.* Even small children manage that. But in this illustration the children put one fan next to another in such a way that all the folded edges pointed to the centre. This is a game of adding elements. The fans are pinned to a soft base. The children used good quality coloured paper from old magazines. They can work in teams or individually.

11

3a

3b

of them properly with such small hands? If we try it with several older children, we can compare the various ways in which children handle the newspaper and what the paper can stand up to. Then we can exhibit and discuss all the various ways in which the children used the newspaper.

One child just crumpled up the paper and turned it into something like a snowball, threw it up and caught it several times, rolled it and then put it back on the table. Another child, as if ashamed, tried to straighten the paper again. Of course this was no longer possible, but an interesting, variously bent and crumpled surface was obtained. Perhaps the child may have noticed that the surface of the newspaper was crumpled rather chaotically, there was no rhyme or reason to it. On the other hand some children folded their paper into four and then crumpled it up. When they opened it out again we all tried to find out whether there was any regularity in the creases. All four areas were crumpled in the same way, some in a mirror image.

There are many ways in which to fold a sheet of paper. The best illustration for this is the Japanese *origami*, the art of folding an endless variety of shapes from a square piece of paper. Origami is roughly a thousand years old and not just a children's game. But even the smallest child can manage to fold a paper hat, or a boat. If we ask children to shape newspaper in any

3a *This time the more complicated fans were made from layered soft paper.* Sometimes the small designer gradually rolled up or bent the separate sheets, pinning them together at the edges. The creative intention is the same – we could also find several points, centres, where the lines met. Older children are able to cope better with this job.

3b *The layers of sheets are spread in space*, their fascination lies in the regularity of arrangement and the converging of the lines – the edges of the paper. It is interesting to observe the shadows they throw in light shining from several angles. Before putting aside old magazines, the children should play with them, for example by folding the sheets regularly in various ways to the axis of the back.

12

4a *Butterflies* in their crysalids have folded and crumpled wings. The smaller children tried this out. They carefully crumpled up soft white paper. Then they placed it on a base of stiff paper and watched how the paper straightened and resisted the crumpling process. Then they dipped it in a dish filled with diluted glue, crumpled it up and shaped it, modelling it into the area of the hard base. Their task was to stress the axis to which the wings of the imaginary butterfly were directed.

4b *This is similar work*, but the crumpling this time has a different, less converging character. The axis is emphasised far more by the crumpled area of the paper. To give greater expression to the very interesting structures and to make them more visible, the children covered them with various chalks when they had dried. Since the background was also rather dirty, they used coloured Chinese ink to paint it.

4a

way they like, they usually fold it in regular pleats like a fan or a book. They go on dividing the folded format in half till it becomes impossible to continue. When they try to straighten the paper out again they find that the traces of the folds are in a regular pattern. Ask the children to describe the pattern they have made, to describe what it looks like – a butterfly? a mirror? a house? an engine? The newspaper folded into the smallest possible format was as thick as a log.

4b

The children could use old discarded timetables for games with paper shapes. Even placed this way in front of us they are worth looking at.

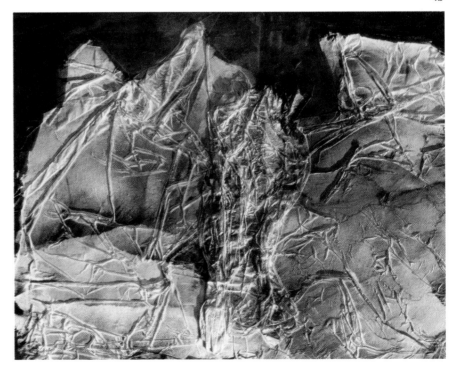

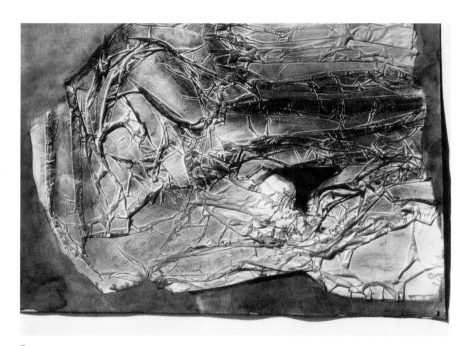

5a

5a *An older girl wanted to make a pleasant shape of crumpled paper.* She proceeded in the same way as in Picture 4. She thoroughly rubbed pink and grey chalk into the crumpled surfaces with her fingers; she regarded this as a great improvement.

After all, we have whole bookcases full of such blocks of layered sheets at home. You can see the magic shapes that can be created from layered, folded paper in Pictures 2, 3a, 3b.

Some children, quite unexpectedly, created a shape from the newspaper by wrapping up boxes or mugs; others wrapped their hands or their head. Some of them tore small openings in the paper for their eyes and looked through to see what the onlookers thought about their 'sculpture'. When the children carefully unwrapped the objects, or parts of their bodies, they found

5b

5b *The unpleasant shape of the crumpled paper* differs widely from the preceding work. How did the artist proceed? The soft paper does not adhere closely to the base. This shape is almost threatening. Or does it want to swallow us? The colour is reminiscent of a dirty puddle. Where the child used black and brown colours the paper looks charred.

14

6a *The dialogue between these two shapes is harmonious.* The larger shape seems to pay court to the narrower one which bends trustingly towards it, gently touching it. This is the work of an older boy who fulfilled his task well and according to his own interpretation.

6a

that for a while the newspaper retained the shape of what had been put into it, or at least some mysterious indication.

Even those who tore the paper into shreds or some kind of fringe contributed to the different methods of giving shape to the flat surface. Some used scissors and produced fringes consisting of threadlike strips. Two boys had an unusual idea. First, they squeezed the newspaper lengthwise and then twisted it as if they were wringing out washing. When they tried to straighten the paper again the result caused considerable surprise!

6b

6b *Danger.* Here the child also fulfilled the task well. The small shape cannot escape. Perhaps the larger one will bite it. At the moment it seems to be yelling at it.

15

7

7 *Snow-covered mountain range.*
The children first slightly dampened the paper and base in diluted glue. Then they lightly placed the thin paper on the base and played with it. They pulled out separate mountains, entire mountain ranges and snow-covered peaks. The paper dried comparatively quickly and the 'mountain' shapes remained. The children then tried to indicate the most interesting 'tourist' path that would take them along the ranges, into the valleys and to the highest peaks. Then they tried to draw the mountain massif from side-view on separate paper.

Some children combined several methods of shaping the newspaper, others used only one. Let us look at the various shapes and try to divide them according to the effect they have on us. Could one establish which newspaper was torn by a 'fearless and daring artist', which was carefully folded by a child who dislikes disorder and untidiness and is usually careful and disciplined? Some newspapers were evidently folded by future designers, since they managed in such a fast and on the whole accidental game to construct rather a complicated and solid shape. But it is not very reliable to attempt to deduce

8

8 *The map of stones* was the result of a simple experiment. The children found interesting stones, coloured them with thin tempera and carefully wrapped them in white paper. They squeezed them in their hands so that the colour from the stones was well imprinted on the paper. The illustration shows the result of the experiment. Could you guess whether the stone had a complicated shape or was smooth?

9 *From a collection of semi-precious stones.* In the museum of semi-precious stones smaller children were given the task of remembering one beautiful stone so that they could draw it on paper, both by shape as well as approximate colour. Our illustration is supposed to recall an agate.

9

from an accidental and immediate reaction when shaping paper a valid conclusion as to the character or the mood of the young designer. It would be better to discuss the character and mood of the shapes that were created.

Let us recapitulate the possibilities of shaping: crumpling, folding, layering, wrapping, tearing and splitting, cutting and twisting. We must also bear in mind that the paper used was medium thick newsprint. The result of applying these methods would be different with softer or very stiff paper.

10

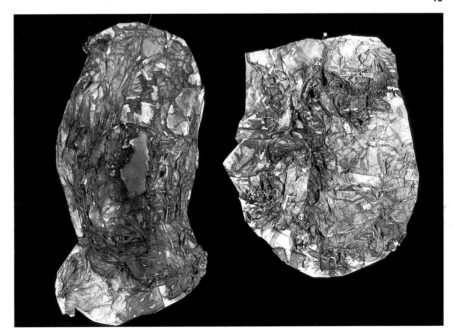

10 *The children were fascinated by amethysts.* They could not manage the regular crystals, but they were careful with the violet shades. They first worked with thin paper dipped into diluted glue and then colour.

11

11 *A maze of shapes.* Looking carefully you see that the illustration consists of two pictures – the work of two children. The photographs are placed next to each other. The maze was formed by turning, bending, folding and layering the paper. Both children had one sheet in front of them, an area which they could not reduce and that was not allowed to disintegrate.

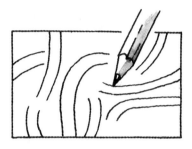

The children first adjusted the paper by cutting into it in different directions. Before they started to work, they had to imagine how the strips would be shaped.

In Pictures 4 to 10 the children worked with white and very thin paper – some used discarded paper from the office. The work was limited already by various set tasks as indicated in the captions to the illustrations. The children added a new method by working the paper 'wet'. They dipped it in diluted glue, placed it on stiffer sheets of paper and sculpted it.

Whatever material the children use and whatever the method of three-

12

12 *The arbitrarily creased paper may remind the children of a barking dog or a cat*, easy to see with a little imagination. We know that this is not difficult for the children, they easily visualise such transformations and name them. For example the sky where huge fantastic cloud formations float is often like some large picture book. In the following chapters we encounter with the ability of children to discover fantastic plants, animals and figures in various objects.

13 *The children blew up three paper bags* of the same or different size, and then carefully shaped them by squeezing them. They represent a 'family' – father, mother and child. We can place the animated bags side by side and think up other situations. What would the situation look like if the three were fighting, whispering to one another, doing exercises? We then use the group as a model and the children can draw it with a soft pencil.

Can you see how an ordinary paper bag can turn into a live monster? This one is caught in the cupboard doors and wants to scare somebody in the dark passage. (More later about modelling with paper bags.)

13

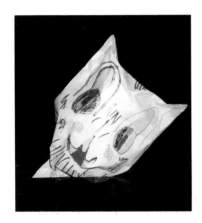

dimensional shaping mentioned in our book, their creative expression will be more convincing if they work with interest and individual courage and inventiveness. Copying some model, following a previously given 'pattern' and set process of work cannot be regarded as the child's work. In spatial creation this danger of imitation can be avoided if we keep in mind creative work, not needlework or handicrafts in workshops. Copying models is not dangerous in drawing or painting as long as the children do not mechanically outline or fill in the pictures in children's colouring books.

Why is only some of the children's artwork convincing and original? Perhaps because some artists have managed to transfer to the viewer the tranquility or tension of the creative means they used in their own individual way. They managed to arrange parts of the shape to give the whole a certain captivating force so that the viewer cannot remain indifferent. The shapes may talk quietly and peacefully to each other, one seems to protect the other, or they support each other.

In a creation of opposing moods there is chaos, the shapes fight, one tries to escape the other, they are afraid of each other. In another attempt there is order, but kept so strictly and geometrically regular that we are relieved

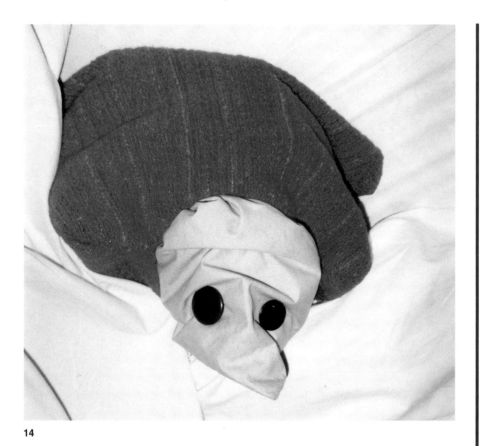

14

14 *Everyone likes to try out model-ling with a pillow*, perhaps in the morning after waking up. Here the child succeeded in producing a fat smiling hobgoblin. We can transform it into a huge hungry chicken, as the small photograph shows. If we add another pillow and a stuffed T-shirt, the child can model any shape in a rapid game of transformations. To preserve some shapes we can use a few rubber bands or ribbons to tie the pillows.

We can use large buttons to indicate eyes. The soft shapes are easy to draw and lightly shade.

when it is unexpectedly disturbed, the shapes are set free and begin happily 'to hop about'.

The illustrations in this chapter show some possibilities of composition, that is, various aspects of 'creative reflections' on chaos or order and equi-librium. Likewise the following chapters do not attempt anything but the devel-opment of the children's ability to think creatively – as clever and inventive designers, sensitive dreamers, or kind-hearted imps with untiring fantasy. Boys, with help, will probably prefer to look for other materials such as stiffer paper, boxes, wooden sticks, wanting to try out their technical abilities in the construction of fantastic flying machines. A child that is nearer to nature, plants and the world of fairytales will be more likely to reach for softer materials such as textiles, plasticine or natural materials like moss, small twigs or fruit. Chil-dren showing technical talent may perhaps refuse to see a mythical dragon in the creases of a featherbed or in the cloud floating across the sky. But it would be a pity if they were not even tempted to do so and stubbornly refused to see anything more than a cloud they might be angry with for hiding the sun.

Let us go back and investigate the shapes we noticed when crumpling newspapers. Let's look at it another way. If we observe how children behave in a shop when surrounded by many different things we realise that people do not only select with their eyes. Are we coming up against the atavistic longing of the hunter and collector to 'reach out and taste'? Is the material soft enough? Is it soothing, as if caressing us, is it crease-resistant and malleable? Shall we feel as if we are wrapped in cottonwool? We want to try and taste the pastries on the dish and smell them at the same time. We must

15a   15b

15a, b *The stone towers hold mysteriously together.* The children competed to see which tower would be the highest. They used plasticine between the stones. This is a small but important exercise in judging stability, balance, even the ability to 'feel' the size, weight and shape of the stones. Not every stone can stay put in a certain place in the tower or support another stone. Our stones in the introductory chapter represent and recall natural material that children like to model with, or arrange side by side. What are they? (Conkers, acorns, rosehips, bark, twigs, small pieces of wood, a bundle of leaves, straws or hay, fruits, melon, orange, marrow or their peels, etc. And naturally the unsurpassed wet sand, snow, clay...)

try on the shoes to find out if they pinch, if they are too loose, and so on. Consequently it is quite natural that we want to ascertain all the qualities and properties of the shape by using all our senses.

Just as we are tempted to pick up a beautiful apple and enjoy pressing our cheeks into a soft pillow, so we daily instinctively try many shapes by touch, their consistency – weight, size, surface and suitability for easy grasping. Without realising it they soothe us, touching them subconsciously excites us. That means that there exist objects in our surroundings which are a joy to stroke, to handle, but also things that repel us, that are unpleasant to the mere touch or that do not affect us at all. We find them on our table, in the closest surroundings. Let's try it, let's shut our eyes and very carefully grope with our hands, with our fingertips for objects that we may feel are 'suitable for stroking'. Have you found them? Maybe it is a spectacle case or the smooth surface of paper. Let us recall one interesting factor connected with the enjoyment produced by touch. There are few adults who can resist picking up a conker when they see it shiny and smooth lying in the park. The longing to hold it has stayed with us from childhood.

Let us try to invent and prepare small 'touch' games for the children. The first creative task that springs to mind is to make (on the principle of worry beads) a 'worry egg', a pleasant shape to put into a pocket, a shape that would soothe us when we rub it between our fingers. The children could find a pebble or make a small velvet cushion or carefully smooth a small piece of wood, no bigger than can fit into their palm. It might even have a groove, an interesting unevenness which we involuntarily examine in our pocket and trace with a finger. After a time we will have assembled a few of these objects. Then we

16

can sit down round the table with the children and gradually, with our eyes shut, test all the shapes and give them points for 'pleasantness'. Which worry bead or egg got the most points and which the fewest? You might see these worry beads at an exhibition of Japanese toys. In Vienna you can find them among the artistic objects in the Hundertwasserhaus. And in Prague? They are sold as 'feelies' for massage or acupressure of important pressure points in the palm.

You probably also know other 'touch' games. When there are more children and adults together, we blindfold two of the children and the others hold out their hands to be examined. Which of the children first guesses correctly the hands of all the men – father, grandfather, brother, schoolfriend? It is worth finding out how the hands of men, women and children differ.

Another game using touch is the arranging of stones in heaps according to size, while blindfold. If there are no stones at hand you can use buttons, little pieces of wood etc. In another variation of searching and arranging the children can compete while blindfold to build the highest tower using building blocks, or to pull out their own cap and shoes from a pile of clothes. Another variation could be the children trying to dress one of their friends while blindfold. But of course, they mustn't have any help!

Various types of loose materials can be differentiated using touch only.

16 *Building* – plastic modelling clay for children – plasticine usually comes in small boxes containing a set of ten different colours. If the children are each given one box they can participate in a simple game. Five 'builders' sit round the table. From the sticks of plasticine they must construct an interesting building, a house with five rooms, or a playground with climbing frame, etc. The interesting part of the game is that they are building blindfold. When it is their turn, by gentle and careful touch the children find out what has changed in the structure, they examine the whole shape and decide where to place their own piece. There is no limit to the variations of this game. For example, each builder may have an adviser who can see, but who is not allowed to actually build, only verbally instruct the builder. The children train their memory for shapes, their imagination and their ability to touch objects gently and get to know a simple construction by touch only.

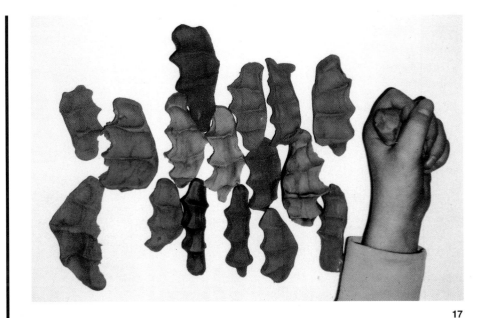

17

17 *What does a 'Nothing' look like if we squeeze it?* The children easily find out the shape of the space in their palms when they firmly squeeze a small piece of plasticine and then let go.

In small flat boxes, or bottle tops, let the children determine by touch only what the material is (rice, poppy seed, semolina, caraway seed, etc). Or guide the children round the room to differentiate various surfaces. We place their fingers on a mirror, the wall, a rug, a carpet. We can mislead them by letting them touch an object that was not in the room before (for instance a towel, a basket or a doormat).

If we are with the children in the woods or a garden we can find out how gently they can touch moss, grass, the bark of various trees when blindfold. We can let them determine by touch only flowers or leaves of trees they know, the bark of birches or firs. It is also worth a try to cover objects with a thick

18

18 *Observing and joining* the imprints from both palms may inspire quick modelling. The orange 'head of a cat' is actually two pieces of plasticine squeezed in the left and right palm and then pressed together. The eyes were formed by the left and right thumb.

19

scarf or a box, examine them with one hand and draw them life-size with the other hand.

The children should feel the shape and its surface thoroughly, say out loud how it affects them, what it reminds them of. Touching something blindfold can be turned into a puzzle for the other children. They write down the clues and exchange notes, for example: 'It's smooth like a wall of ice, but it's not as cold as ice. It's upright and my fingers jump over tiny little paths. I go up and down them with my finger and suddenly they cross. It is like the plan of a field, flower beds... It's the tiled wall in the bathroom.'

20

21 *Quick modelling* on a can, flower-pot or some old dish has several advantages. The children save plasticine but achieve work of larger size. When the round shapes dry they often remind the children of the heads and bodies of animals or fantastic creatures. They only have to model the eyebrows, eyes, characteristic mouths and noses. The plasticine adheres comparatively well. The vessels can later be cleaned easily in warm water.

22 *Imprints of beads* in a thin layer of plasticine encourages a number of minor activities testing surface and shape. You can introduce a number of rules. When they have a chain of beads we can ask the children to print them in a certain order (in regular rows, curves or spirals). Then they reflatten the plasticine layer and print the beads in interesting disorder as shown in the illustration.

21   **22**

Or 'Ouch, ouch, I felt a tiny prick. It's like a little ball. I must stroke it gently and slowly, otherwise it may hurt more. It doesn't move, it's not a hedgehog or an armadillo, not a fork... it's a small cactus.'

Antonyms, opposites, should not be missing in a child's vocabulary: soft–hard, round–angular, blunt–sharp, smooth–rough–granular, whole–artic-ulated, regular–irregular, symmetrical–unsymmetrical. The difficulty some-times of putting into words impressions received by touch can be tried out with older children. Let them differentiate in words between similar rounded shapes:

23

23 *The imprint of a piece of wire netting* was made during a walk. The children had some plasticine with them in a plastic bag. They spread out in the park to look for an interesting structure which would leave a strong imprint in the soft material. Then they met again and tried to guess where the others had found their imprints. Another task to set the children is to ask them to find something that would leave a perfectly regular imprint in the plasticine. When they bring their finds we show them that by repeated shifting or crossing the imprint of one flat twig they can also obtain a regular pattern.

25

24

24 *The imprint of the inside of a shell is very beautiful.* The children called it a disc 'recording the sound of the sea'. It reminded them of petrified prehistoric plants and animals. They enjoy being left on their own to prepare a small exhibition of 'fossils'. They simply take imprints of interesting plants, combine them and add to them. Then they describe their fossils. They invent fantastic names, the period when the plant existed and describe its interesting characteristics.

an apple, a coconut, an onion, an orange, a tennis ball, a tomato, a cabbage, a potato. Would the children be able to draw them in approximately the same size only by touch and indicate the structure of the surface that they could feel, again by touch only? Would they be able to model them in plasticine?

We have tried stroking the uneven surface of an object with closed eyes, but can the children recognise its imprint (actually a sort of negative) in plasticine, what an interesting surface they are dealing with? So we can play another game. Every child takes a piece of plasticine about the size of his or her palm. We decide on a certain area, whether the kitchen or part of the garden. There the children walk about for a while and unobserved by each other take the imprint in plasticine of an interesting surface (the grain on a plank of the gate, the surface of a doormat, the bark of a tree, a washing line, the top of a watering can, etc). The children then place their 'finds' next to one another and try to guess what imprints the others have taken. The imprints could also be sorted according to whether they come from nature or are a manufactured object (mortar, tiles, doormats). Many imprints could also be drawn. One could compare the difference in the drawing of the actual model and that of its imprint. Older children can collect their particularly successful imprints in a shallow box and cast them in plaster of Paris.

With the younger children we can work with plasticine for a little longer. It is suitable for quick playful work and also readily available. If we add to it, in the course of time the plasticine gets mixed into a general grey colour, like

25a *The imprints of a cheese grater* are combined into a new system. As in the original object so in the imprint the axis of symmetry remains, but what fills the new shape differs from the model. Only after the children have tried out several variations do they decide which is the best, and then we help them to cast it in plaster of Paris.

25b *The dialogue of the clothes pegs* is interesting because the coloured pegs do not speak, their imprints speak for them. Since their imprints are quiet, organised and perfectly formed, their dialogue is very serious, truthful, almost scientific. Can you imagine what the imprints would look like if some of the pegs where to lie, to quarrel or to laugh at the others? What would the whole surface of the plasticine look like if all the pegs were to quarrel or even fight?

25a   25b

sculptor's clay. Plasticine has innumerable uses. When playing and determining shape, or modelling directly on objects, we often do not want to preserve anything permanently.

At first the children can play with small sticks of plasticine (see Pictures 16, 17, 18, 19, 20). They need a plastic tray in front of them, a small dish with water to wet their hands so that the plasticine does not get too warm. If this does happen, put it in the fridge for a short while or outside the window, if it is cold enough. There are many more simple 'touch' games. For instance, who can make the longest snake from the same quantity of plasticine without tearing it? Who can manage from three pieces of plasticine to produce the

25c

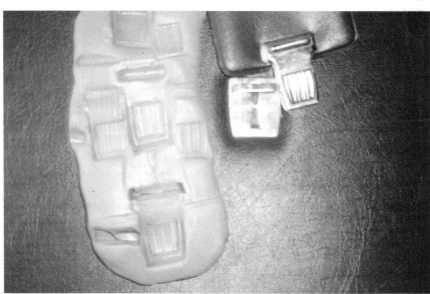

25c *The lock of an attaché case* could tell us how often its owner presses the catch and opens it every day. The plasticine gives a printed report, a kind of sculptured evidence. Can you imagine in what excited 'shape' language your pencil would talk, the door knob, the zip, the water tap?

27

26

26 *Scaffolding* made from the children's drinking straws offers structural possibilities that we shall meet again in Chapter 5. Plasticine is again the binding material for the base. We can push a number of small pieces of wood, straws or spills into it like the spikes of a porcupine. We remind the children of the invention of this type of engineering structure in technical industrial buildings and point out the role of the reinforced concrete. When we walk with them past similar structures on which huge cranes are at work, we remind them of these 'hollow' constructions.

A pot of coloured straws or wooden spills is not only a decorative object. It should be part of the teaching aids for creative modelling.

roundest three-coloured ball by rolling it between the palms? Which child can model the most beautiful and, as far as shape is concerned, the most eye-catching 'lollipop', or sweets to put in a box? Who can squeeze out the most beautiful and colourful 'nothing' (Picture 23)?

Then we can use a round coloured pencil or felt-tipped pen like a rolling pin and roll out a piece of plasticine to the size of our palm. Then look around for a small hard object which we can press into the clay – first the whole and then part of it. Let us imagine a key that wants to show itself in all its beauty and from all angles, show us what it can do and so tell us about itself. Or could we show the imprints of two keys on a piece of plasticine, how they seem to talk to each other, have a debate, perhaps even quarrel. For the time being this is only a game. We smooth out the piece of plasticine again and again. Then we try to put the imprints into some sort of order. We can arrange them in a circle, into a spiral or along an axis. We can work with deeper and shallower imprints. We can show some tool in motion in the surface of the plasticine. What can scissors do for example, what does the pressure of pincers look like or a clothes peg? How does a fork behave?

We can also use plasticine as binding material. It works well for a time to hold together stones (Pictures 15a, b), spills or pieces of wood (Picture 26). The children can model some objects in plasticine, for example mugs or flower pots (Picture 21).

I have not been able in this chapter to mention and illustrate all the available materials suitable for spatial creation. I shall mention a few more in the following chapters. Very suitable for instance are seemingly useless materials such as assorted boxes, remnants, wires, newspapers, melon skins, fallen leaves, etc.

Try to judge these things as sculptors would or puppeteers, illustrators, inventors, humorists and think: 'Could I build a house or a maze from these boxes? Do these coca cola bottles remind me of a submarine, a ship or the body of a dachshund? Could I hang painted bottles that are not too heavy on

27a *We shall play a game with the straws* similar to the one we saw in the illustration of the 'stone tower', but requiring far more delicate touching. There is a similar game which comes from Japan. Every player has the same number of spills. We place them one after the other over the rim of a mug, trying to make an interesting structure. We can alternate horizontal and vertical positions. In our illustration the players had to avoid pushing the spills into the mug, so that they avoided vertical directions which are riskier.

27a

a tree to represent fruits – or sausages? Just look, isn't that large paper sack a sculpture in itself? It might be enough to crumple it up a bit more, or to add some colour'. Pablo Picasso drew inspiration from things that he accidentally found, *objets trouvés*, such as the handlebars and the saddle of a bicycle. Marcel Duchamp chose a bottle drier as a sculpture for an exhibition without touching it any further (ready made). Chapter 4 deals with the grouping of objects which have accidentally come together to create poetical, and sometimes ridiculous and provocative still life.

27b

27b *Which clumsy engineer knocked the structure down?* That small boy got as many bad points as the number of spills he displaced! You will see how important it is to have a steady hand for the gentlest, finest touch, how you have to imagine the mechanical load of the various straws and test the possibilities of your new, more interesting construction by adding a further structural element.

29

A Tree bark most probably reminds the children of an old man's wrinkles, a freshly ploughed field or tightly plaited string. Let us try with the children to stroke it while keeping our eyes closed. It is by touch that we learn to communicate with a living tree. We can imprint various kinds of bark into soft plasticine and then guess which tree it comes from.

B Children have discovered some green tree bark in a shaded and damp place in a park. They try to clean it with coloured chalk. A much more distinctive texture appears resembling plaited string.

C The hand by sculptor Olbram Zoubek reminds some children of pine bark, others of a swallow's nest. The children conclude that the sculptor modelled a coarse-textured statue by adding cement piece by piece; light refracts and shimmers as it falls on the surface of the statue.

D Enormous coils of rope varying in thickness can be found at Viking's, a small Prague shop whose owner is obviously a former sailor. The wound-up ropes stand there like enormous tree stumps, barrels or wasps' nests.

A

B

C

D

E F

E   Boxes of small polished semi-precious stones make you want to play with them. The stones are lovely and smooth. They rattle in a box as if chattering to each another. Like rainbow drops, purple amethyst, pink and white crystal or rose-quartz, red cornelian, yellow jasper, lapis-lazuli, lazurite and turquoise, green-moss agate or malachite and black-grey haematite run through your fingers. Even the brown-yellow tiger eye can be seen glistening.

F   A pavement of ordinary pebbles looks most interesting in the rain. How long must it have taken a patient river to polish them down to their rounded shapes?

G   *Ivan Novotný* (born 1958), *A metal iron object*, 1992, 4 cm in length. Can you imagine how big and dangerous a giant dragon would be with sharp claws like these? Just one of these spikes weighs 1000 kg. (The student struggled like a brave knight to complete this dissertation work. He forged it at an ironworks under the guidance of sculptor Kurt Gebauer, Professor at the University of Applied Arts in Prague.)

H   *Ivan Novotný, A metal object*, 1992, weight 1500 kg.
'Look, a giant has pulled out a thorn from his heel!' – 'Oh no, this is a fishing-rod for the biggest fish in the world,' argued two children in front of this monumental sculpture. (This herculean work of art was created by a student in the studio of sculpture under the guidance of Professor Kurt Gebauer at the University of Applied Arts in Prague.)

G

H

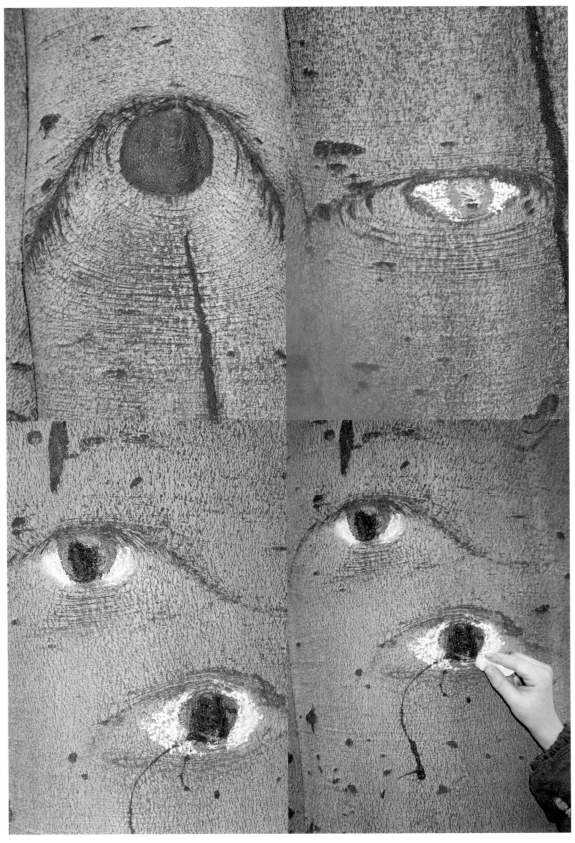

Contact with Nature

Contact with trees. Paper beetles. Were there dragons in prehistoric times? Playing at prehistoric cave artists. Oh, to be a bird for just a little while! Interesting tetrapods. Animal masks.

Every creative activity is based on recognition, experience and memory. Story-telling is part of it, too. We'll start this chapter with the topic 'tree'. First take the children to see some trees. Take with you coloured chalks, Chinese ink, white and coloured paper, string, rope, plasticine, etc. You are in an orchard, a forest or a park and assume that the children have already some knowledge of and emotional experience with trees.

You are sitting in the meadow, the children around you and you say: 'Close your eyes for a bit and remember the tree that you liked best. Can you tell me why?' After a while the children start to tell you – their eyes still firmly shut – about a tree, a pear tree, on which their first swing was fixed. Once curtains blowing away, caught on the pear tree and it looked as if it was getting married. You may find out that the boys prefer nut, cherry and chestnut trees. These are the ones they enjoy climbing. One of the boys fell off and he can still clearly see in his mind's eye the branch that broke under him. One little girl tells about a weeping willow, one of the boys tells about a tree with a beautiful hollow where he used to hide his treasures. Another child picked apples with her grandfather and recalls that the branches nearly touched the ground

28 *How do trees look at us?* The smaller children set out for a walk to one of the oldest parks of the city, to have a good look at the trees. On the beeches they discovered 'eyes' and this reminded them of the fairytale in which a girl changed into a tree. Is that her? The knots on the beech – a boy made the eyes more expressive by colouring them with ordinary chalk that rain would wash away again. He waited to see whether the 'eyes' would notice the casual passers-by. Our illustration is a photo montage of four shots.

29 *The children discovered mysterious holes* in an old pear tree that seemed to lead to the soul of the tree or were calling out to us. Are these perhaps blind, extinct eyes? Or are these holes secret entrances to the lair of some creature inside the tree? This is a small creative contact between the child and the tree made visible. Blue chalk rubbed in emphasised what the child found most fascinating and worth thinking about. The creative 'interference' is negligible, the children know that the first rain will erase all traces of the chalk on the tree.

30a

30b

and one could hide under them so well. Try from where you sit to observe the trees around you, whether any of them looks interesting even from a distance. Tell each other what you see. The lovely grey bark of the beech has an interesting design. Several small seedlings – tiny fir trees – have sheltered under

30c

30a *The tree – a friend?* For their creative contact with nature the children brought with them plasticine, chalk, coloured paper, string and ribbons, bandages, 'hands' cut out of paper and also white and coloured felt-tipped pens. This is the same tree and holes as shown in Picture 29 and the same small artist. This time the tree is trying to make friends with people and reaching out to shake hands with them.

30b *The tree – an enemy?* The picture is proof of how the holes left from branches attract the children, they are almost afraid to reach into them when they are very deep. Try it yourselves, perhaps 'something' will grab your inquisitive hand. Just look, in the picture a dangerous creature hidden in the tree is unsheathing its claws. This is what creative contact with a tree can also look like. The children made the green claws from plasticine.

30c *Have we the same eyes as the beech tree?* A shot of the boy's eyes and the 'eye' of the beech completes the illustrations of creative contact with trees. The tree that catches our attention can first be drawn, its changes then photographed throughout the year. We can build an interesting nest in its branches, add some differently coloured leaves, decorate it for Sunday, etc.

31a, b *Trees – babies.* When the trees, in this instance conifers, are still small, they are just as delightful as all young things. Have you ever noticed small plump firs? They look like bristling kittens, they wear prickly, curious bonnets, they look like snowed-under white dolls. So it is not surprising that the children wanted to model them, especially at Christmas time, when small firs are an endangered species in the Czech Republic. We have made small paper shapes from layered paper rings that the children threaded on wooden spills and then stood in a lump of plasticine. They first worked out how to express simply the prickly small branches of the conifers. Light and shade alternate in interesting patterns on the layers of fringed paper.

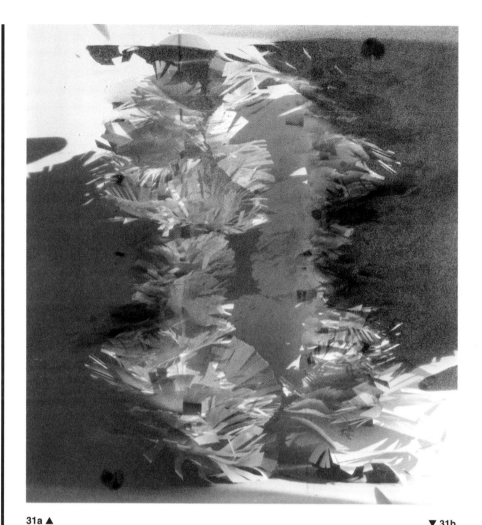

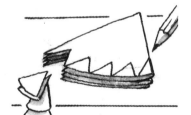

31a ▲   ▼ 31b

32

32 *A small park.* These large leaves dropped from house plants. First we put them under a sheet of glass. There they dried flat. Then a boy drew on them with felt-tipped pens and stood them in lumps of plasticine. He added other dried plants and thus created a small stage set. The trees are turned sideways like stage props. Wouldn't you like to try that when the leaves are falling from the trees in autumn? Before creating a park from flat leaves check outside whether the outlines of the crown of a well-grown tree are similar to the shape of its leaf (as is the case with maple, linden and poplar).

the green tops of the tree stumps. Where is their mother? Which tree has the most beautiful trunk and which the straightest?

And now everybody begins making discoveries. Children will try to find a tree they can 'communicate with creatively', a tree that attracts them by its branches, crown, bark, fruit or growth. Through this creative investigation the tree makes a lasting impression on our memory and we will be able to recall it at any time, even if 'our' tree has succumbed to the woodcutter's saw. When

33

33 *This fantastic landscape* also looks like a stage set. Before the children produced this work they had seen the Prague Quadrienale, an international competition of stage sets and costumes held in Prague every four years. The children tried to create fantastic landscapes as stage sets, composed of animals, various imaginary plants and parts of a landscape. All flat and shaped parts of the sets were selected and cut out from suitable reproductions in magazines and calendars. The children added their own drawings or paintings to the sets.

34a, b *A carnivorous plant* is unique and thus surrounded by mystery. Even though the children knew that such a plant would not bite off their fingers, their drawings and models were of a somewhat threatening character. Both these photos of blossoms are actually large orifices – mouths with dangerous teeth that only pretend to be flower petals by their colour. Two boys produced these spatial objects from two similar parts which they glued together. Simplified designs are shown in the sketch.

34a

we are looking for our tree and creative communication with it we must not hurt it, any creative interference on our part must easily be washed away by a spot of rain.

Let's see what the children might come up with, what such a creative communication with the tree might look like. For instance the children may use some chalk to underline the knots (Pictures 28, 30a) or other unevenness in the bark or on the tree stump, dry branches, etc. With the aid of string or

34b

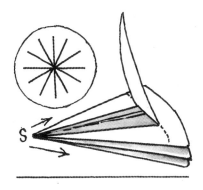

35a

coloured threads one child weaves an interesting 'spider's web' on the lower branches. Another uses coloured string to show where a squirrel could hop along the tree, or a woodpecker. The little fir tree had a birthday and in celebration its branches and top were decorated with fringes so that it looked like a Christmas tree in the middle of summer. The oak suddenly had strange blue, violet or orange leaves among its real green ones. They were made of coloured paper and they seemed to suit the oak. One of the trees fell 'ill', a child wound bandages round it. A few table-tennis balls fixed to the beech brought curious people from afar to see what strange fruit they were. If the conditions are suitable, the children can investigate the size of the tree crown very simply by drawing lines into the sand or with chalk on the asphalt path to outline the shadow of the crown and then indicate the largest branches. If you are in the

35b

35c

35a, b, c, d *Fantastic beetles.* The photograph shows that the children cut the base for the beetle from white paper folded along the vertical axis. From coloured paper, but also from suitable parts from colour magazines, they gradually superimposed onto the white 'body' of the beetle coloured eyes, wings folded lengthwise, and across them smaller coloured elytra. To make the beetle spatial they put stiffened folded legs under the body, fluffed out the wings and elytra, and sometimes they glued the whole beetle onto an oblong paper box. You can read more about insects in Chapter 2.

park long enough, the children can draw the shadow of the tree crown with another coloured chalk so that they realise that every tree can indicate the time just like a sundial. Every tree measures the hours every day even if nobody's watching!

Not only one chapter but a whole book could be dedicated to the tree. An investigation of trees and all that belong to them could assume different creative concepts and variations. The book would certainly be interesting but should not be taken as a 'cookery book full of recipes' for imitation. Art education (including that which covers only one topic) should stimulate the children to independent creative thought, to variations of ideas and to further discoveries. It is never purely mechanical imitation. Further creative activity might refer only to flowers, or to the artistic investigation of prehistoric animals, birds or fish. And all the time we are still only within the sphere of animate nature.

In this chapter I will introduce sculpting from paper with the subject of 'investigating insects – beetles'; I discussed this in the first book on creative activities, but concentrated on drawing. So let me show that the motivation of both activities, that is both sculpture and drawing, is closely connected. The children should have a good look at illustrations of beetles and collections in the school's natural science laboratory. They could find out for themselves how many types of insects scientists have already discovered. The interesting things that the children come across in their investigations are also part of creative motivation. Who would not be interested to know that ants live in ant

36a

hills, how various types of spiders use their webs, which beetle is the largest, which the smallest, how praying mantises or grasshoppers behave? It is important for these creative activities that the adult know that every insect has a perfect body structure and that this is why so many variations occur. Every insect consists of a head containing the organs of sense, eyes, feelers, mandibles, the thorax to which all organs of motion are attached, legs, wings and elytra. The third and last part is the abdomen containing the digestive and reproductive organs.

36b

36a, b *Were there dragons living in prehistoric times?* If we link a dragon in our imagination with some reconstructed giant lizard, the answer is yes. The scientists are still arguing why all huge species of lizards died out about 65 million years ago. But the children saw the reconstructed skeletons in scientific literature. They drew them with Chinese ink and wooden sticks. The most difficult part was to draw the joints. The models of the giant lizards are much smaller than the children's drawings. They are braced in the trunk and limbs by spills. In scientific terminology the dragons would be called *Ornithosaurus, Brachiosaurus, Tyrannosaurus rex.*

40

37a, b, c *Altamira* is a 280 metre long cave in northern Spain, its walls covered with paintings from various periods of the younger Palaeolithic Age (*palaios* – older, *lithos* – stone). The children learned that prehistoric people made use of the uneven stone walls which reminded them of animal shapes. Sometimes they even used stencils of bark or skin, so that they could produce a positive or negative image of a horse's head (outer background). The children worked by creasing dark paper and observing its inequalities as if they were dealing with a rock. They tried to visualise their animals. They drew them and tore them out, making a stencil for the inner and outer cover (positive, negative) and then they went to work on the 'rock wall' – large paper. They worked with charcoal and soft red pigment. Finally they glued the tornout horse onto the paper. The illustrations show details from the large surface of the paper.

37a

If the adult does not explain this, then the children's drawings and spatial creations will only be superficial. Remember how children who have seen a butterfly many times happily draw (paint or spatially construct) butterflies with wings attached like huge ears to both sides of the body, because they do not realise that the wings grow out of the thorax, a comparatively small part of the body. The children should know this. We are dealing with the intricate and perfect structure of the insect's body given it by nature. Even if the

37b

37c

41

38

39

children think up new types of insects, each new bug should be structurally logical. It must always be a bug. Its wings and elytra must not remind us of the fins of a fish and it must not lose its 'buglike' character.

Another great opportunity for creative artwork is prehistoric animals. They offer the children – and the scientists – the same opportunity for fantasy and guesswork. Fantasy always fills in the blank spaces between concrete proofs. What has remained, for instance, of the dragons or the legendary giant lizards? – the reconstruction of skeletons in palaeontology museums, drawings, animated films depicting *Ornithosuchus*, the oldest scaly predator, the herbivorous giant *Brachiosaurus*, the strange runner *Ornithomimus* that looked like an ostrich and stole the other lizards' eggs. None of them survived into the Tertiary, they became extinct sixty-five million years ago. Children love to search for and collect material if they suspect some mystery. Even our giant plasticine lizards photographed on the windowsill (Pictures 36a, 36b) are due to a small fantastic reconstruction of extinct fairytale dragons. What does it matter that the children first drew the large skeleton of an ordinary hen which they borrowed from the natural science room? They have to find out for themselves how the bones and joints of the legs and upper limbs are fixed to the trunk, what the vertebrae look like, the breastbone, etc. The children enjoy covering the skeleton that they have drawn with a 'coat' of feathers or fur. They can then model their drawing of the giant lizard in plasticine. The soft shape can easily be braced with wooden spills. At the time when the giant lizards lived they did not have their 'portrait painters' but the mammoths, bisons and horses were better off 20,000 years ago. However, human beings in the depths of their caves and by the gleam of primitive rushlights did not draw or etch animals for amusement or to 'decorate' the cave. This was hunters' magic. They probably drew each animal only once and then 'killed' it with a stroke

38 *A strange horseman.* The figure of the rider and the fantastic shape of the horse were found in the folds of the creased paper. The children who looked for and then tore out their animals for Altamira worked in a similar manner.

39 *An elephant or perhaps a mammoth.* If prehistoric man had seen a rock shaped like this, he would have drawn the outlines of a mammoth on it. One of the younger girls discovered the likeness of the animal on creased paper, which she also crumpled up between two flat sheets of stiffer paper, one of which she had covered with black and blue colour. If you were to turn the mammoth upside down, maybe you would see another animal.

40a *One of the younger boys produced the wild pig.* The children had to model an animal shape from the creased paper and glue it to a dark base. They had to exaggerate the typical features of the animal. Here the boy chose to exaggerate the fangs. They are even larger than the front legs. Prehistoric people seem to have done the same. They stressed what they were most afraid of, what they had to watch out for during the hunt, or what they considered important. The children had a week to decide what animal to choose.

40b, c *Crumplieses.* These fantastic animal shapes were also made from crumpled paper that the children layered. Then they continued to wrap the shapes and wind coloured threads round them. Fairytales and legends are full of fantastic animals.

40a

before the actual hunt itself. For the next successful hunt another animal had to be drawn on the wall of the cave. Whoever managed to depict the mighty bison so that it appeared even more threatening than in reality soon gained the respect of the group, and perhaps did not even have to go hunting but became the 'medicine man' – in short the painter of magic animals. Introducing children to illustrations of cave paintings in Font de Gaume and

40b

40c

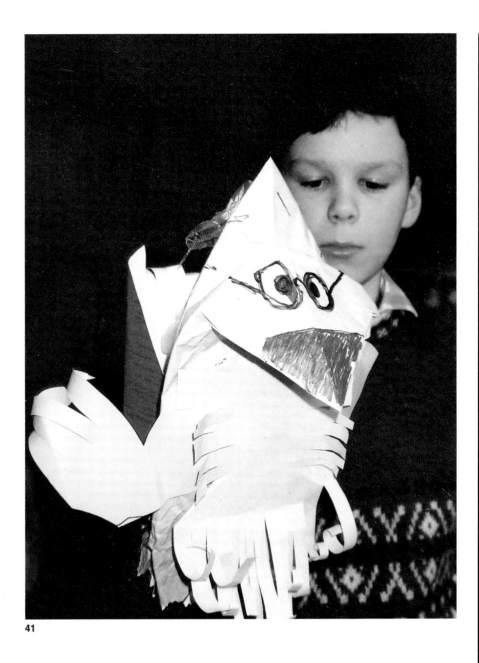

41

41 *The parrot or cockatoo* was photographed together with its creator. The boy placed a paper bag in front of him on his desk, as you can see in the photograph. He quickly finished the eyes and beak, but took great care with the wings. He cut them out from paper in pastel shades.

Lascauz, France, or Altamira, Spain, encourages independent creation (see Pictures 37a, 37b, 37c, 38, 39, 40).

Let's discuss magic a little longer. If you ask children which animal they would like to be transformed into for a while, they very often mention birds. Flying presents mysterious possibilities, tempting advantages. But when you remind the children that as birds they would have to sacrifice their upper limbs, their arms and hands, they are somewhat taken aback. For it is a fact that vertebrates with six limbs do not exist except in legends, such as Pegasus, the winged horse, or the Centaur. The legends also tell of unusual birds. It is worthwhile, together with the children, to look for further information about the giant Noh, the holy Ibis, Phoenix rising again and again from the ashes. Could the children explain the proverb 'Don't carry owls to Athens'? (Quota-

44

42a *White baby crows.* The children found it easy to make birds from paper bags. It was sufficient to paint two eyes onto the white bag, colour the beak and to indicate the wings with chalk marks. Too little is sometimes better than too much. One child painted over the whole bag and the expression of the bird was lost in the colours.

42a

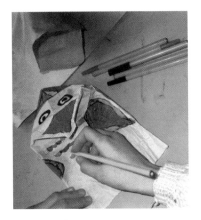

tion from Aristophanes's *The Birds*, meaning, 'Don't carry coals to Newcastle'.)

Still on the subject of birds, Pictures 41, 42a, 42b show a simple little game with paper bags that is sometimes successful in creative activities. When the children were playing with the bags they put them on their hands, blew them up and held them together at the bottom. The corners of the bag were the ears and so one could model a cat from it. But how surprised they were when they turned the bags round with one corner pointing towards them, turned the other one down and suddenly found that this reminded them of the hooked beak of a parrot. When they turned the other corner up they found

42b

42b *The parrot family* on the windowsill is colourful but still full of character. It is a simple idea, a game, simple puppets for a fairytale. For example, the magic chick has to be hatched from a black egg. Only then will the chick help to fulfil all its owner's wishes. The children twisted a rubber band around the bottom of the painted bag and pressed a piece of plasticine into the 'foot' – formed by pulling apart the paper below the elastic. Then the bird could sit down anywhere. It even always landed on its feet, however high it was thrown into the air. Well, a magic chick!

43a

43b

that they had created some sort of a parrot's or a rooster's crest. Then they opened out the bag in front of them leaving the corners folded as the photo shows, and finished off the bird puppets with coloured pencil or felt-tipped pens. A group of birds threaded on spills could be placed outside on the lawn, a small fence or a branch. They present a cheerful, charming sight and even the very small children enjoy looking at them.

Equally surprising are small birds with their wings spanned wide, as in

43c

43a *Parrots or humming birds are almost unknown to the children of Central Europe.* What they do know about them comes from interesting stories and pictures. But when we know only a little we can give our fantasy free rein. There is interesting literature dealing with the food and life of this tiniest of all birds. And it gave the idea of making an aviary filled with tropical native plants for exotic paper birds. The illustration shows details of the aviary and the diagram shows the simple method we used to make the shapes.

43b *The owl* was made by one of the skilful older girls. She started out with a round box – a shape similar to that of an owl's head. All other parts (beak, wings, body and feet) were added gradually. She didn't have a pattern, only her own clever hands and a spatial idea of a simple puppet.

43c *The keeper of the exotic birds* created one of them himself. As far as dimensions are concerned, however, are they large pigeons or perhaps the Phoenix?

46

44 *The ragbird* is the work of one of the smaller boys. The base of this fantastic bird is a coca cola bottle covered with a sock. The children have the most surprising things in their boxes. When you search through several of them you begin to wonder what these perfectly good old gloves could be used for, plastic wrappings from fruit (bird's eyes), or a fringed paperchain (tail). You still have to work out what to fix the puppet on to make it appear natural in space. This one is fixed with three strings to a longish piece of wood.

Pictures 43a, 43c. Whereas the birds made of paper bags were alike in shape, you can see that these small parrots or humming birds have different heads and crests, vary in size, the shape of their bodies, and in the interesting solution of their wings, tails and beautiful tail feathers. People say that the humming bird is a flying jewel in the jungle; the colours of the bird's wings must remain elegant, pleasing and never loud and common like the motley colours of a fairground. If we compare the construction of a humming bird with that of an aeroplane which the children attempt in Chapter 4, you may notice certain similarities. The wings and the tail are perpendicular to the axis of the body. The

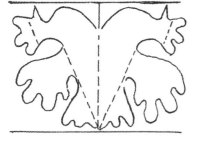

45 *This fly* has a wing span of 50 cm. It was made in the same way as the preceding ragbird. The boy searched through the boxes till he found beads from an abacus and freezer wrapping. Then he got hooked on the idea of making a fly.

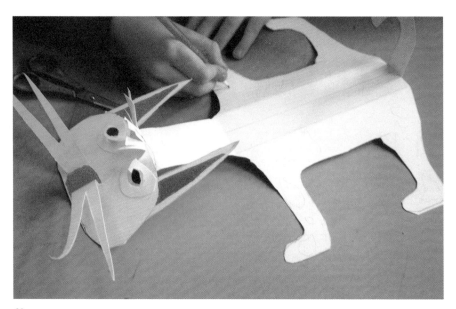

46a

46a *A cat.* This spread-out cat 'skin' is the basis for all further four-legged animals that differ from each other only in the proportion of their legs to body and head. If the body is longer and more cylindrical and the legs shorter, then you are more likely to get a dog, a dachshund. Longer legs with an almost square body probably belong to a good runner, a deer or stag. Although it is evident from the one fold on the spine of the cat that it was cut in one go, the children had to allow for a flat back which is given in this animal by the width of the neck.

children also based the construction of two puppets on this principle – a fantasy bird (Picture 44) and a large fly (Picture 45). The main axis for the first was a coca cola bottle and for the fly a ruler wrapped in paper. During assembly (in our case stitching and tying) the children should decide whether the bird puppet will hang freely or sit on a branch. It should also be interesting when viewed from below, if that is the angle from which it will be seen best.

An entire zoo can be cut out and folded from paper. Every animal skin can be spread out flat like the pattern pieces of a dress. But the skin of the cat would not fit a hedgehog and that of the hedgehog would not suit a rabbit, and so on. Let us imagine that we are tailors, not dressing people but making well-fitting clothes for animals. When looking at the flat sheet of paper the

46b

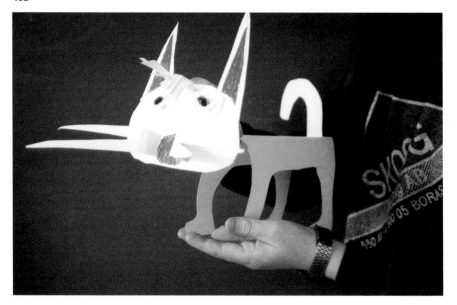

46b *A cat on all fours* held by its creator is proof that the children had no pattern for the animals shaped in this way – which are rather designs for simplified puppets or toys. But they were told to imagine the spread-out skin of the animal, its 'packaging'. The lateral view is decisive, however, and we can tell what animal it is. Not even in Altamira did prehistoric man draw horses or bisons from above, from in front or behind.

48

47 *A black panther cub.* One of the older girls created a puppet, the design for a toy. If the head is comparatively large in relation to the body you have a young animal. This is because the flat skull bones grow far more slowly than the quickly lengthening leg bones. That we are dealing with a toy can be seen also by the exaggeration of the stripes on the body.

child must be able to imagine the animal from the side, from above, in short its skin in plan. Let us look first at some of the children's 'favourites', very often a cat or a dog. We'll try to stroke it. We watch the movement of our hand. When is it horizontal? We stroke the dog from its narrow muzzle across the head, neck and spine almost to the point of its tail. Could we draw the dog from above, that is the central part of its pelt? If we stroke the dog down its sides with both hands, we see that their position is perpendicular (to the central part). These are then the two vertical parts joined to the horizontal central area. Illustrations from an encyclopedia or a book on animals may be helpful. For the simplified coat for the cat or dog the children will need two mirror images of lateral drawings, between them the strip of the central part for the spine. The best way to produce the head of a cat or tiger facing us is shown by the spread-out skin of a cat in Picture 46a.

Smaller children find it easier to make a little animal from one or two boxes. The children can glue a head with ears (and also horns) onto one box, as well as wings or a tail. It is probably better to cut the legs directly out of the box. If the children decide to use two boxes, they make the head out of one and the body out of the other (see the owl, Picture 43b). It is important to estimate the proportion of the head and body and the children ought to be given a wide choice of possible combinations from a large assortment of boxes. These should be ready on the table together with some animal illustrations before work begins. Let us try with the children to draw only with the ratio of two squares of different size an elephant, a lion, a hen, a dachshund. The

48

48 *What is possibly the first meeting of town children with a calf is instructive.* The children have a far better knowledge of animals from the zoo than of the creature that gives them their daily supply of milk. The photo shows 9 to 10-year-olds in nature class.

head of the hen would fit into the smallest box and its body into the largest. In the case of the lion with a thick mane the proportions would change, for the body of the dachshund we would need a longish box, etc.

Should the children want to model a stork, a giraffe or a horse, they have to think how to make the characteristic longer neck. Small children have no difficulty in gluing coloured paper onto the boxes or painting them. If they succeed in creating a fantasy animal or a creature combined from the parts

49

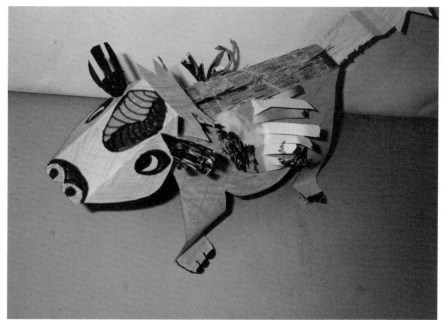

49 *A flying cow as a kite* or possibly the likeness of the Minotaur? Not at all, this magic cow has to have wings to manage the delivery of all the cream cakes, milk chocolates, yoghurts and the pints of milk daily consumed by the children. This is how the children expressed their thanks to the animal.

50 *The merry spring lamb* at first 'did not even know that it was an animal'. Since artists and children are granted a certain amount of freedom, this animal got its name only after one of the younger girls had thought that because of the curls on its large ears and the shape of the head it might indeed be a sheep. And 'spring' because it's so cheerfully coloured.

50

of several different animals, they not only like to invent a name for it, but also a short character description. They will tell you where the animal lives, what it feeds on, how it builds a nest or shelter, how it would behave if it could be tamed. Pictures 50, 51 show two fantastic animals.

Finally we'll make one of the children's favourites – masks. To dress up, especially disguised as animals, has a very long tradition confirmed by fairy-tales, old legends, fables and ballads, where people changed into plants or

51

51 *This armadillo* is also a fantastic animal. The small artist knew that the stripes were different on a real armadillo, that it did not have a red head, green snout and blue socks on its feet. But I ask you, wouldn't you like one of them in your zoo?

51

52a

52b

animals. This was either as punishment, a curse, or it was in some way an advantage to them.

Very often a human being spent the day in the likeness of a swan, frog or deer, but at night was allowed to change back into a human. This is how people identified with nature; they believed that their closest relations could well be plants or animals. They honoured them, they told stories and legends about them. To give visible expression to this similarity and a possible transformation they did not hesitate to execute magic dances on the occasion of various feasts and to dress up as animals and produce stylised masks recalling their characteristics in simplified form.

As early as 15,000 to 10,000 years ago a prehistoric hunter depicted a man dancing and wearing a mask on the walls of the 'Trois Frères' cave in France. He has horns and probably also a horse's tail and a skin thrown over his shoulders. The children are sure to remember some adventure film or stories about Red Indians or other primitive tribes. They would probably have seen a totem pole, the representation of several animals protecting their tribe. The Indians held some animals in such high esteem that they tried by some heroic deed to gain the right to bear their name (bear, bull). They also used animal masks for ceremonial dances.

The masks in Pictures 52a, b, c, d show that the children did not imagine the animal heads too realistically. These are the artistic representations of the characteristics of a dog (the long ears in Picture 52a). To make the dog more frightening the eyes are painted as if flames were issuing from them. Even the horns show that the dog is special and has some supernatural powers.

The children enjoy making their masks in secret hideouts. What is the magic of a mask? Its sudden appearance, that we do not have the slightest inkling who hides behind it? In the cultures of the African and Pacific nations

52a   *A dog with fiery eyes* might look like the devil, but if you recall Andersen's fairytale *The Tinder Box*, then the largest of them surely looked like this. This is the mask of a fantasy animal that children love to make. They fold a large square of paper in half. They sketch where to place the holes for the eyes and especially how far apart they must be so that they can see through them easily when they put on the mask. Then they work out how to simplify the eyes and make them more expressive, then the long nose and ears, horns or antlers. Plenty of fur round the face is not a bad idea either. The children worked with wax crayons.

52b   *The dog princess.* This mask is quite different from the large mask covering the whole face. The girl also knew how to dress when wearing the mask.

52c *The devil with large curving horns* belongs to the species of plump lazy stay-at-homes that will never get on in hell. Even in the fairytales everybody gets the better of him.

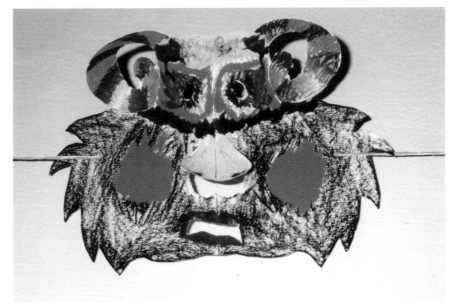

52c

the real hero in the festivities is the mask of the honoured animal and never the man behind it – and so let us believe that it was a 'fiery dog' that barked at us and not our own son!

52d

52d *The lion was pink and pale blue* halfway through the work. The small artist hardly knew what to do, for nobody was afraid of it, although the mask had an important task to fulfil – to represent the bewitched prince in *Beauty and the Beast*. Finally the artist got hold of a brush and outlined the mask with dark colours to give it more emphasis.

53

A

D

▼ C   ▲ B

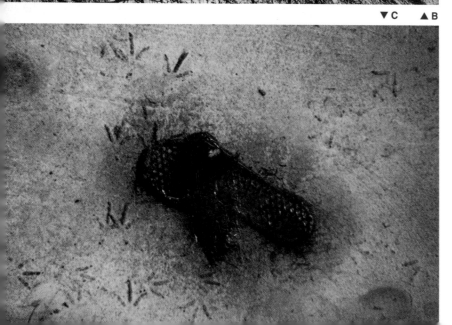

A   A 150-year-old giant died in the oldest Prague orchards – now Chotek Park. When people felled the tree, it seemed even bigger and scared the children. They could not decide just how old it was when trying to count the rings. Its huge stump is like a large circular stage resembling an enormous gramophone record which the children would love to listen to and so find out what the tree had witnessed in his time.

B   An enormous griffin which flies in the rain and storm was discovered by children in the wintry crown of the old birch tree. They wondered why the thick branch had to grow in a different direction. The thin twigs reminded them of drizzling rain, the hair of a witch or a fine cobweb.

C   Human tracks intersected by bird tracks preserved in a concrete pavement. Who was the man? Is he still alive? What were the birds like? What were they looking for? Similar questions are being asked by palaeontologists about the imprint of a track made by a theropod, a three-toed carnivorous dinosaur who became famous for simply walking in clay by the River Paluxa in Texas.

D *Veronika Zapletalová* (born 1971), *Snake*, 1992, coloured textile, height 250 cm. Does this remind you of the serpent from the Garden of Eden? The tree here has also become an integral part of artistic expression. (This is a student's work from the Studio of spatial textile art and alternative techniques under Professor Adéla Matasová at the University of Applied Arts, Prague.)

E The more aggressive of the two shells, the one with the claws, wins the struggle between two shapes. The other, shaped like a mouth or ear, is furtively lying in wait. Even the shadows in the picture book are threatening. Both the large mollusc shells, the Spider Conch (*Pterocera bryonia* Gm.) and the King Helmet (*Cassis tuberosa* L.) caught in the Indian Ocean, have found their way to children who play with them, sketch them and model them.

F *Vladimír Syrovátka* (born 1938), *Earphones for listening to the sounds of the sea*, 1987. Items which would appear not to relate can be combined by certain people into entirely new humorous or poetic reality. Surrealists and Dadaists enjoy doing this even today.

G The rhinoceros tends to be depicted in old drawings almost as a knight in armour. Its 2-cm thick skin tends to be divided by folds into some kind of plates. It resembles prehistoric animals, looking unyielding and sullen in its clumsiness and lack of shape.

H A rhinoceros assembled from squares of paper demonstrates how Japanese origami manages to deal with the proportions of the head, legs, horns and ears.

E

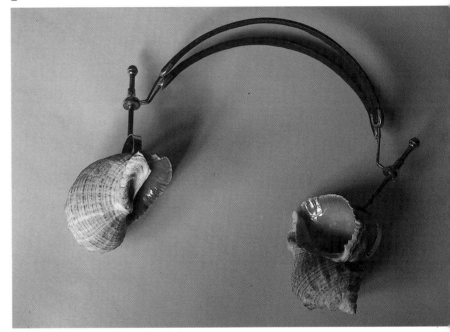

F

G

H

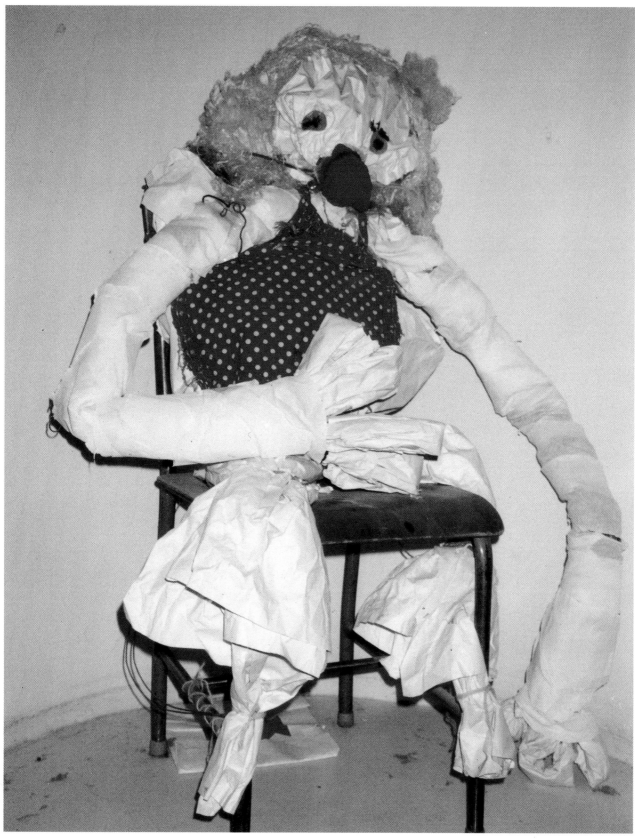

3

How Nature Modelled Us

Plasticine figures with movable limbs. We examine our own hands. Leafing through our own head? Different masks. Helmets and hats not only change the shape of our head. Hoods and overalls – empaquetage (wrapping up) of the human body.

If the children can draw the reduced world on small sheets of paper, why should they not also be able to model it as shown by the mannikins in Pictures 53 and 54? In this chapter the children start out from the normal size of heads, hands and figures. They will act as their own models.

The same proportions are valid for the full size and for the reduced human figure as proved by any photograph. But people do not usually look alike. The fatties differ from the trained athletes, but they, in turn, are different from slim or skinny people. The twenty-six types of human figures mentioned by Albrecht Dürer (1471–1528) would confuse the children. Michelangelo (1475–1564) judged the human body by the size of the head, which should amount to one eighth of the total body length. Leonardo da Vinci's (1452–1519) advice is probably the simplest for children. Divide man into four parts: 1. from the top of the head to the chest; 2. from the chest to the hips; 3. from the hips to the knees; 4. from the knees to the soles of the foot. Using a ruler children enjoy measuring their own bodies. But they can also cut out some upright figures of men, women and children from old magazines. These can be folded in half and in four and they find that the sitting figure is shortened by one quarter, just as much as a kneeling figure. They discover that men usually have wider

53 *The white figure* was made by layering, twisting and constantly rewrapping paper. Three girls made it from several parts which they tied together with string. They then tied the whole figure to a chair. Why has it got such long arms? Well, of course, because it loves all the children and wants to hug them!

54 *What can be done with a slipper, an iron or a bottle* to pose mannikins in various positions and situations. They first carried the slipper, then they turned it into a boat or a big slide. This is how animated films are produced; the little figures are photographed in various phases of the movement. And quite often the animators use soft sculptor's clay to create their mobile actors. The malleability of plasticine is fairly similar to that of clay.

55a

55a *Inquisitive hands* can stand in space like a sculpture, but they can also be hung up like a mobile to recall even more strongly the constant activity of the hands. Some people will be reminded of a tree when looking at this shape, its branches also reach out into space. The sketch shows how the children worked with the layered paper.

shoulders and narrower hips than women. It seems that all young creatures have something in common, they have large heads. This is caused by the disproportion of the child's head to the body. As the child grows the body grows much more quickly, the long bones extend faster whereas the skull hardly grows at all.

Children enjoy drawing pencilled outlines of their friend's prostrate figure on a large piece of paper. When they cut it out they can check the proportions by folding the paper. It is interesting to outline the figure of an adult in chalk on a wall. Then the smaller shape of a child can be drawn inside it or beside

55b

55c

55b *Touches and gestures made visible.* The children cut out paper hands, coloured them and placed them in space. The hands touched chairs, door knobs, waved out of the window, jumped out at us from a cupboard, inquisitively crawled into the room through half-open doors, stroked a tree, leafed through a book, peeped out from under a blanket, typed on the typewriter. The children attached them slightly to the objects with glue or a tack. Together with the object, for example the typewriter, they formed an interesting sculpture.

55c *This head of a particularly good boy* shows his mother's caresses – gaily coloured hands cut out from paper.

58

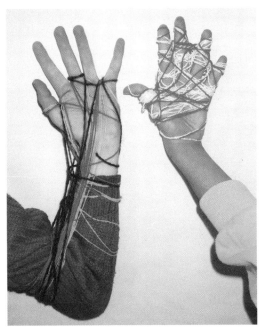

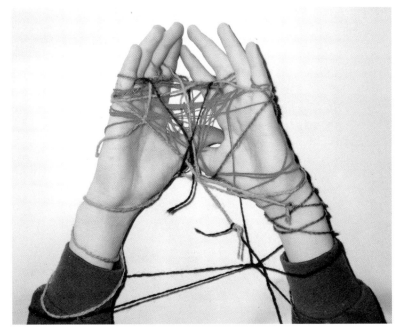

56a   56b

56a *Spider games.* How can we
ascertain the shape of our own
hands? The children had several balls
of cotton thread. They tried to find out
what they could 'draw in coloured
lines' on their hands, and express
creatively. It was important that by
winding the thread regularly round
their hands they became aware of
their shape. Some of them pretended
to be a spider, others looked for the
secret lines in the hand where your
'fate' is supposed to be written.
Others pretended that they had made
visible the veins and nerves of their
hands, and others said that they were
knitting mad gloves.

56b *The spatial relationship
between their two hands* – the
children had to work this out on each
other. Some did this by stressing the
symmetry of their friends' hands.
Others tried to upset it.

it. The text to the illustrations describes the modelling of small figures in plasticine. The children broke the braces – wooden spills – into four parts (crown
of the head, chest, hips, knees). But the small figure must always be checked
from the side, in case it is too flat. Do not stop children from modelling directly
from the cut-out or outlined 'model'. The aim is, after all, to recognise the
proportions of the human body and, with the soft modelling material and wood
bracing, they can model and construct figures in various positions, move them

56c

56c One of the boys tried to test on
himself the spatial relationship of the
arm bent at the elbow to his body and
differentiated the various directions by
coloured threads.

59

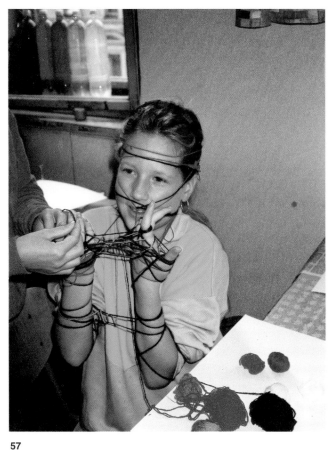

57

58

as if they were fighting with each other, exercising, crawling over a shoe, turning the handle of a little coffee grinder, moving a mug, handing us a pen, creeping into our pencil case, etc. 'Arranged' like that the children enjoy drawing them with wooden sticks and Chinese ink.

If the children are eager to try out interesting movements of the little figure they can imagine it positioned on their left hand. The index finger is its right foot, the thumb the right hand, the head would be somewhere in the bend of the wrist. Using both hands can you make this little figure trip along the table, sit down or kneel?

It is worthwhile investigating your hands separately, they are the most ingenious features of the human body. They manage for instance to 'pinch', that is to place the thumb against all the other fingers. This is what makes us humans. The gestures depicted in Picture 55b show everything that we can manage to do with our hands. Can you name some typical actions? We stroke with our hands, we weigh objects, we wave, we salute, we threaten, etc.

We can verify the shape of a hand or the whole human body by bandaging it or drawing round it – empaquetage, also part of the field of plastic arts. Man is actually a large walking parcel. Why? Because every day we 'wrap ourselves in textiles' – our clothes. What if our summer clothes were suddenly to march out of our wardrobe! And if the children stuff a pillow inside their nightie or pyjamas they can see themselves as fun figures. People are daily, every second and during every movement – measured. How? By a tireless thread.

57 *Composing both hands and head* and trying to indicate the axial symmetry of the human body. A working photograph.

58 *How to fetter Gulliver.* The boy first drew his hand in the middle of a sheet of paper and then partly cut it out and flipped it up. To keep it fixed in space in the same position he tried to tie it in the same way you put up a tent (there are slits cut in the edges of the paper). Those of you who know Swift's *Gulliver's Travels* will realise what the boy in the picture had in mind. Concentrating the ropes on three points only might increase the strength of the entire structure.

59 Two spiders? Or a quarrel made visible? Both boys wound thin threads round themselves to ascertain the spatial relationship between them. The black-haired boy was the more active.

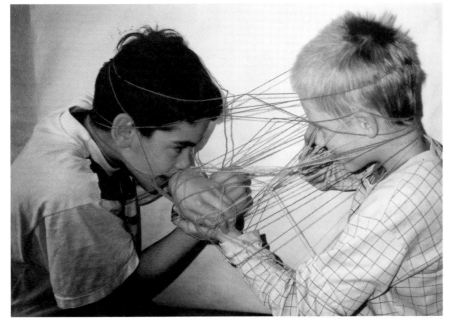

59

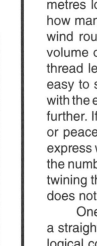

The thread in a shirt knows exactly the distance from wrist to elbow, and the size of the human chest spanned by the shirt. With a thread about twenty metres long we can play an amusing game during which we can measure how many somersaults a friend turned on the meadow. By a thread that we wind round a friend or round ourselves we can easily find the length, the volume of the human figure and parts of the body. And not only that. If the thread leading from hand or head into space catches on some object, it is easy to see the direction of the movement, the communication of our body with the environment. But let's take our three-dimensional considerations even further. If two friends wind the threads round each other, they can by the wild or peaceful arrangement of the threads and their colour scheme creatively express what sort of conversation they are having. For example by increasing the number of threads (as well as the lines on a piece of paper) and their inter-twining they can show that one talks more than the other, quarrels or shouts, does not let the other get a word in edgeways.

One communicates directly, in straight lines, the other tries to avoid a straight answer, talks round the subject, pulls the other's leg and prevents logical communication. Can we imagine how to draw a conversation in two or more lines on a plane, could we manage it by arranging threads in space? For smaller children this is an interesting way to discover form and shape. They can tie up their left hand only with coloured threads in a certain order. Children the whole world over know games with threads which by various lifting off and slipping over the hands produce amazing shapes. They decide, for example, to take a red thread along the lines on their palm. They begin, perhaps, to weave it in and out of their fingers in a regular way till their hands look like the 'webbed feet of a water fowl'. They may remember how the tiny inhabitants of Lilliput discovered Gulliver sleeping and quickly tied his hands to prevent him from hurting them. Picture 58 shows the various ways the children tied up their hands.

Interesting work can be done by modelling with stuffed pieces of clothing

61

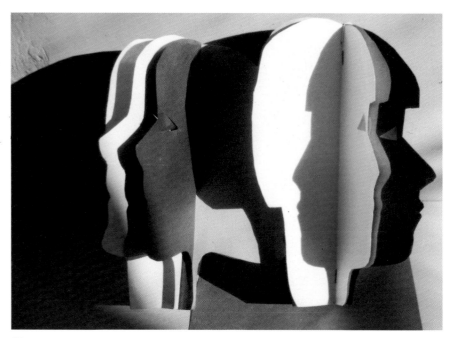

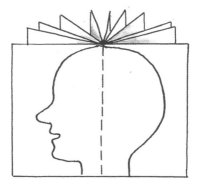

60a
60b

60a, b *My head – a register.* These paper shapes are made in the same way as 'Inquisitive Hands', Picture 55a. The profiles of the heads correspond to reality. The children first drew the shadows of their heads on paper, or placed their heads on a sheet of paper and let a friend outline it in pencil. The sculptures of the heads varied greatly, the artists bent and turned the paper heads or completed them with pencil lines. The profiles became very interesting when they threw elongated shadows under various lighting.

62

61 *Masks from aluminium foil* which the children modelled directly on their faces. When they took the masks off they made holes for the eyes and mouth. Then they modelled various facial expressions, yawning, weeping, shouting, laughing. These two masks are singing a love duet.

61

such as tights or gloves. Imagine what fun could be had with a sculpture made of stuffed multicoloured gloves tied into a huge bouquet. Then the children could search for a suitable place to display it, perhaps by tying it to a tree. It would turn in the wind like a huge prickly fruit or a giant seed pod, or it could walk like a huge porcupine in the grass. Or what if the children were to place the huge bundle of gloves on their head like a fantastic hat?

But best of all children like to paint and draw heads. They are interested

62

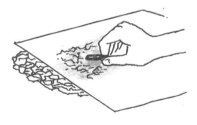

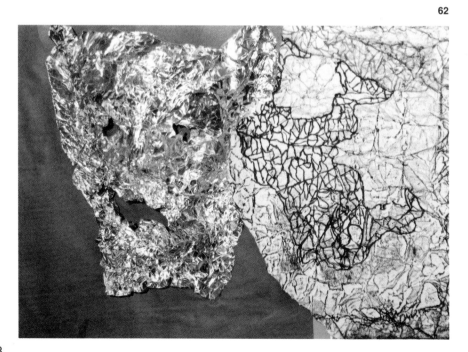

62 *A mask and a record of its 'wrinkles'.* Interesting wrinkles form when you crease foil. The children try to draw them freehand, or take a rubbing with crayons (see diagram).

63

63

63 *Bearded Grandpa.* A younger child was working with soft paper dipped into diluted glue. He first placed it on another sheet of paper and then 'pulled Grandpa by the nose'. And the glue preserved its shape. The eyes and the beard are formed from another piece of paper dipped in glue.

64a *The mask of a shaman* to call forth the dawn; on the other side of the cylinder is the same mask but from black paper to call forth nightfall. The children also imagined the contrast of white, good and black, evil, demonstrated by the shamans and medicine men. Instead of a real-istic depiction of the face there is the creative effort of stressing the size of the eyes by giving them an oriental shape and the simplification of the stylised nose and mouth. In the museum the children had seen negro and Polynesian carvings.

in the expression of the face, the likeness of a known or imagined person. They have already looked into the mirror and drawn their own portrait. Pictures 60a, 60b suggest that they should try and make a paper sculpture and model the outlines of their own head or profile. Smaller children are better using old colour magazines for such work, because the paper layers are already stitched together. Working in pairs helps. The children imagine that their finished work will depict the 'head of a reader' full of all the interesting things from the maga-zine, and proceed in their work as shown in Pictures 60a, 60b and the sketch.

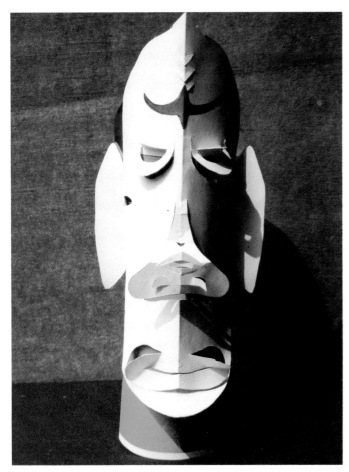

64b

64a

64c

64b, c *The midday witch* is walking round the cottage. This wicked fairy-tale creature may have been invented in Bohemia to make sure that the children never dawdle on their way home which would make them late for lunch. In the Czech fairytales this witch has her male counterpart who is supposed to look like a whirlwind raising dust and sand. They appear at high noon, a time as enchanted and magical as midnight. The children made paper masks of what they imagined these creatures to look like and for a while they walked round the houses with them, then they stuck the cylindrical paper mask of the witch on a fence. An old curtain gave it the appearance of an old woman – a proper midday witch. The masks are cut out of large pieces of paper folded in two. The fold is the axis of the face and can be clearly seen in the opened-out mask of the shaman.

When leafing through the 'magazine-head' the children can stick or draw eyes or a mouth on some pages, or even what the head is thinking about when reading something interesting.

The children also enjoy making their own three-dimensional portrait from soft aluminium foil. When they start thinking up various other different facial expressions we can point out to them that this is what some Renaissance ball masks looked like. The children might also find it interesting that the ancient Greeks more than two thousand years ago tried to preserve the likeness of their nearest deceased relatives. For this purpose they made a wax death mask. During feasts they hired actors who represented the deceased members of their family. In ancient Greece the actors also wore masks on the stage. These were made by specialists from linen stiffened with plaster of Paris. They coloured them and fixed beards and hair to them. The mouth was a wide opening with a mouthpiece attached to it which strengthened the voice like a speaking trumpet. The masks represented certain types of people. For instance, for comedies there were the masks of 'the first and second old man', servants, fat old women, gossips. The mask of the 'dried-up old woman' represented evil. We also know the mask of the 'fire-brand', where the coiffure above the mask ended in a point above the crown of the head. But we only know these masks from their marble copies or from scenes of plays depicted on

65a

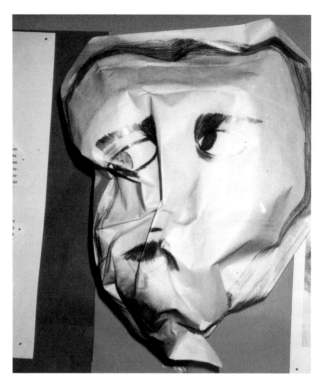

65b

vases. The linen masks have not survived. Women were not allowed to act on the stage. Their parts were played by men with a female mask covering their faces.

In comparing the children's work we find that in the creation of three-dimensional heads two approaches have been taken. In the first case there is an actual realistic likeness especially when the children began their creations from the outlines of their own profile (Pictures 60a, 60b) or from the modelled

65c

65a *This mask of terror* recalls the Czech saying that fear has large eyes. When people are afraid their eyes probably do bulge like this. The boy made the head from a large paper bag, a smaller bag formed the nose which was glued on. Then he painted the face with thick tempera. The brightly-coloured mask of fear is matched by the boy's pullover with a large dentated pattern. The whole seems to express the chattering of teeth and shouts of terror.

65b *An older girl drew a head on a paper bag* and shaded it with a soft pencil. Then she blew up the bag and shaped the nose, the eyebrows and the chin by squashing it. And so the face could take on various interesting expressions. The children were allowed to choose from a number of black-and-white photographs of famous people for their drawings. Here Honoré de Balzac was the model.

65c *The three heads from paper bags* were worked in different ways by the children. They only outlined the first two faces on the left without shading them. They are faces of 'sorrow'. But on the other side of the paper bag the faces are smiling. One of the younger girls glued a colour photo on the third bag which she had

66

cut out of a magazine. When the children pulled the bags over their hands and squashed the paper in various ways from inside they were surprised how the faces came to life.

66 *Two girls are showing masks for shamans and sorcerers.* For the children the distance between the eyes was of importance, so that one could see properly through the holes. They solved the enlargement of the face symmetrically in colour and form, using almost geometrical décor suitable for certain parts of the face, such as rings round the eyes and semicircles, triangles, stripes. The masks were meant to cover almost the whole face, changing it completely. The children worked with broad coloured felt-tipped pens.

66

67a, b *Transformations of the human face.* This time there remained on the face only what can change a person completely. Glasses, eyebrows and a moustache were fixed to an expressive nose. Even the girls could turn themselves into magic old men. The children cut the masks from a folded piece of paper, the fold being the axis of the face.

likeness of their face (Pictures 61, 62), or when they use a face from a photograph, whether to produce a collage (Picture 65c) or a realistic drawing (Picture 65b).

In the second case we are dealing with a head and mask where a rather more decorative approach has been used. For instance the eyes are simplified and magnified. The nose, mouth and cheeks are made up of geometrical shapes. We are dealing with a spatial ornament, geometric rhythm and often

67a

67b

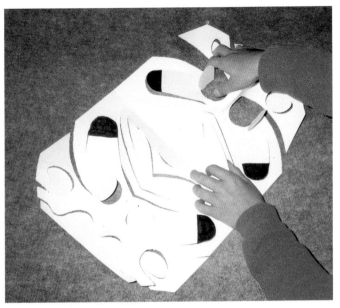

68a

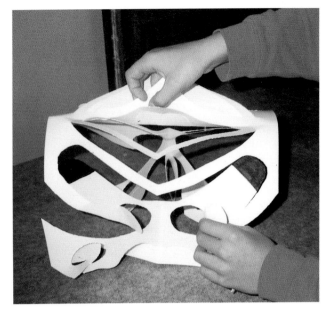

68b

strict symmetry along the vertical axis. The masks recall stylised Indian totems and negro carvings (Pictures 64a, b, c, 65a, 66). This is, however, only superficial similarity. The children producing these masks did not have the same experience as the Red Indians whose deep feeling for their artistic creations is based on an interpretation of the world passed down for generations. Contemporary man always seeks inspiration for the expression of feelings, often turning to ancient cultures for inspiration. When the children worked on masks they were able to attend an exhibition on shamans and medicine men and gained a lot of information, both from photographs and exhibits. Such

68c

68a, b *How to shape a helmet.* The shape laid out flat only started to be interesting when the boy pulled it out slowly from the centre of the piece of paper. He turned it, played with it and tried to put it on his head in various positions.

68c *A fantastic helmet for a fairytale knight* on the head of its creator, who chose this position for the helmet for the photograph. It protects his nose well that way. In knightly tournaments a sword would slide off the ingenious shape. Furthermore, a knight's helmet must also raise terror in the eyes of its beholders and stress the outstanding capabilities of its wearer. The children then drew their fellow pupils with their helmets, adding imaginary armour in the drawings.

68

information may also be obtained from the extensive literature documenting the culture of primitive peoples.

In the interesting publication by the German Professor Julius Lips (1895–1950) *Vom Ursprung der Dinge* (On the Origin of Things, 1954), the chapter on the origin of the theatre stresses the important part played in the lives of primitive peoples by masks and costumes. The Pueblo Indians of the Zuñi tribe firmly believed that their costumes and masks were given to them by the gods, and looked after them with great care, passing them on from generation to generation. They had a separate keeper for them who lived in a special house. There was even the pretence of feeding the masks so the Indians would say 'Go and feed the ancestors!' Only those for whom the masks were destined and to whom they belonged were able to 'read' certain omens from them, for example rain, animals and plants. The adolescent males also had a special subject to learn – instruction about the theatre and the reading of omens.

It is not only with the aid of masks that the children can give their faces another dimension. Before we consider various hats and the changes they produce let us look at protective helmets (Pictures 68a, 68b, 69a, 69b). These are head coverings that in the course of history have not changed their purpose of protecting the head from injury and have therefore also preserved their shape. People soon discovered that nature cheated them somewhat when she did not equip them with a carapace like a turtle or the house of a snail or even the horns and antlers of the noble animals, the strong defenders of the herd. Boys like to enumerate how many protective helmets they know. They usually begin with the knights' helmets worn in tournaments that also bear the emblems of social position and esteem. Some seem to want to terrify their opponent. To those who remember the helmets of the Roman gladiators we suggest a look in the encyclopedia of ancient culture where they will find illustrations and descriptions of helmets. Boys are sure to mention the special helmets of sportsmen and racing drivers and the helmets of fencers. They

The illustration shows the folding of a piece of A3 paper into four parts. On one quarter cuts are indicated in pencil, which always turn round the centre of the folded paper, but are never cut through completely. The whole piece of paper remains together, see Picture 68a.

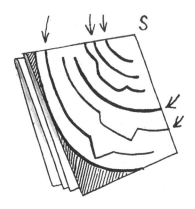

69a   **69b**

69a, b   *Sports helmets* look like cages covering head and face. A ball must not injure the goal keeper. The astronauts' helmets, the boys assured us, may be constructed with radar aerials fixed to them.

70a

70b

think the contemporary headgear worn by the ice hockey goalkeeper or the Formula One racing driver is closest to the medieval knight's helmet. Some are bound to mention that an astronaut must also wear a helmet, but that it is probably fitted inside with complicated equipment and various instruments, also to be found in the helmets of pilots and divers. The boys mention that such a helmet allows breathing, maintains the correct pressure, ensures total sound insulation and perfect two-way communication. With their lively imagination they can cope with additional external equipment (radar, aerials, searchlights etc). The boys can start a picture documentation of helmets from sports journals, motoring magazines and sales manuals, interspersed with their own sketches of helmets that they saw during visits to castles or museums. The children enjoy trying out a few types of helmets and so becoming for a few moments the person that wore it. Picture 68c shows how children behave even if only wearing a paper helmet.

People not only protected their heads from blows, they also covered their heads against cold, rain and sunstroke. Apart from its practical uses headgear also fulfilled the function of decoration, the expression of social position or membership of some professional group. Head coverings were divided according to men and women, age and status (married or single), the historical period and the place on the globe. Just as a well-made shirt or coat changes the human figure, so the hat changes the head and actually also the personality. This is why I included considerations of items of clothing in the chapter on the human figure and not among things that human beings produce for their own benefit. Before the children start to invent fantastic headgear we

70a *A wig and hat* were arranged on a polystyrene head. The model recalls the hair styles and wigs of noble Egyptian ladies, illustrations of which the girls found in publications on the history of art, and also in their history textbooks.

70b *The folding hat for Juliet* was made in the same way as the knights' helmets. The girl turned the central parts up to form an interestingly shaped hat above the coiffure. The side parts recall the bonnets of Renaissance ladies. They were used to restrain thick tresses, veils or nets. If somebody in later times invented a folding top hat for the gentlemen, why should the ladies not have folding hats?

71a   **71b**

71a   *A hat with feather and butterfly* in the style of a turban. The girl in this photograph made it for her friend. The stuffed blue T-shirt is fixed to the head with a yellow ribbon. The second pink T-shirt is freely arranged. The feather and butterfly are supposed to add a touch of frivolity to the rather staid hat.

71b   *Wig and hat.* The girl is wearing an old lampshade on which a tangle of coloured threads has been arranged. The lampshade has the advantage that the girl can arrange her hat on it herself and try it out on her head step-by-step.

encourage them to enumerate all the things people have thought of wearing on their heads. They most often remember: hat, top hat, bowler, sombrero, fez, turban, beret, cap, hood, bonnet, forage cap, coif, fur hat, deerstalker, cowl, straw hat, headband, crown, diadem, tiara, helmet, veil, wig, wreath, headscarf, kepi, peaked cap, flat cap, mitre. In larger libraries there is specialist literature on the development of clothes. Hats have an important place there. They belong to the fashion of a certain period and tell us about people. We can hardly imagine a Pharaoh in a top hat, or an Indian in a diver's helmet. But you can try that in a collage – we can interchange the headgear that we have cut out from magazines and look for a suitable 'victim' to give a sombrero, for example. The more incongruous, the greater the fun.

These activities stimulate the children's creativity, but we can also give them the following somewhat less traditional task: Find in Norbert Lynton's *Landmarks of the World's Art: The Modern World* (1965), some top hats, berets and royal crowns, draw them and write down the name of the artist and the title of the work. Small children, like detectives, searched and found the picture of the *Old King* (Georges Rouault, 1936) and the sculpture *King of Kings* (Constantin Brancusi, 1937). They found top hats and berets as well, of which there were far more. This is an unusual educational process where the children remember the picture or sculpture from the treasure store of world art through a detail and manage to recall it when we speak about it later on.

Feet and shoes are useful when studying the human figure. In the first book on children's activities we dealt with human footprints that show the types of human walk and a person's mood. Children are tempted to draw attrac-

71

72

tively coloured sports footwear. Many of them want to design sports footwear, Cinderella's slippers or seven-mile boots. They can try that with the help of coloured paper, aluminium foil, or plasticine. The design can be actual size or enlarged. Before we start we should, as always, select suitable shoes stitched in different ways. This means that the children can place soft coloured paper over the various parts of the uppers and try to draw the outlines, cut them out and glue the parts together. First simple slippers, moccasins, then their mother's shoes, various types of shoes worn in the house, and finally

73

73 *Design for shoes* – a good test for checking on the shape of one's feet. The children modelled a new shape in colour directly on the old shoe with the aid of plasticine. They can also try it with paper by wrapping, tying and gluing, etc.

74 *Waistcoat with fringes.* Making clothes even if only from paper also helps the children to become aware of the structure of their own bodies. The older children produced simple waistcoats from large pieces of paper. They made their patterns by one of them lying on the folded paper and the other drawing the outline. In this case the children glued on paper streamers left over from the children's carnival. The children had to design a model for a waistcoat that would be unique; you could hardly get material in a shop for this kind of waistcoat.

74

the interestingly multicoloured sports shoes. Smaller children can model their design in coloured plasticine directly onto old boots or shoes, see Picture 73. They could do that equally well with cottonwool dipped into diluted glue. When dry the children can dye the boot with tempera. As an interesting object, an invention, they can add small wings, wheels, a propeller, a paper windmill or spiral springs under the heel, etc. These additions are also suitable for hats. Many fairytales speak of coats, caps and boots becoming part of the magic power of the various supernatural creatures. In Greek mythology the gods not only have wings on their backs but also on their caps and boots (Greek Hermes, Roman Mercury).

At the beginning of this chapter when modelling tiny figures we mentioned the proportions of the human body. We can verify these proportions with the aid of several possible procedures, starting with bandaging the entire body or cutting along its drawn contours. The children already know something about this from their games. They love the first snowfall. They throw snowballs and gleefully fall into the soft snow. Try falling on your back onto

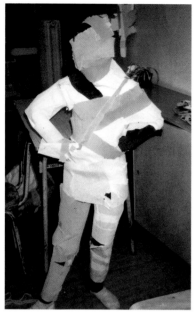

75a

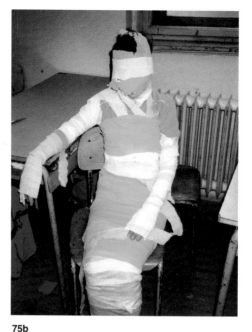

75b

75a, b *The coloured statues* were made of empaquetage, the wrapping up of a friend. The children worked in teams of three, they had coloured crepe paper which they rolled like bandages.

a slope where the snow is undisturbed and sufficiently thick. When somebody helps you up your imprint is very sharp in the snow and the children can compare their own with yours. You can add butterfly wings to the figure by lying in the snow and pressing in your arms, moving them from straight up beside your ears, down until they lie alongside your body. Some children cannot resist this and use small twigs, stores and leaves to add eyes, nose and mouth, as if they were dealing with the negative of a starved-looking snowman.

75c

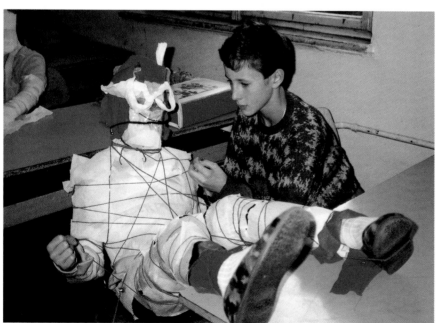

75c *Overalls for a Formula One driver.* The position of the wrapped-up driver shows how he will sit in his car during races. This is how his friend drew him as well. And he added a car in cross-section.

76a *The designer himself adjusts the contours* of his prostrate friend torn out from a large piece of paper. He drew a pencil outline of his friend lying on the floor in an expressive position. When he tore out the silhouette, he tried to show how the figure could change position by folding the paper at the joints.

76a

Children play in the same way on a sandy beach by heaping wet sand round themselves to produce their negative form. They decorate it with small shells, add seaweed as hair, and so on. We can then make up a story – tell the children about a lost boy who lay down near the seaside by an empty conch and turned into a flying fish. Nothing was left of him except the imprint of his body in the sand. It is entirely up to you what other stories you invent.

76b

76b *Placing the figures in suitable surroundings,* here on an old door. The boys not only worked with the silhouette that they had torn out (see Picture 76a) but also made use of the remaining paper, the 'hole of the figure', that is the negative. They called the figure 'The thief and his shadow'. They probably had in mind the black conscience of the thief, which he can never get rid of, just as he cannot lose his shadow.

77   **78**

Just as the children drew the contours of the treetops and observed how their shadows moved on, they can outline their own shadows on the asphalt path or a suitable wall. The shadow figures can fight with each other, embrace or dance. The children like to add faces and clothes from natural products, including grass hair. If they outline their longest shadow, in the evening, on paper and cut it out, it can be folded like a concertina in the joints and shortened to its original size. See Pictures 76a, b. A similar procedure to verify the human figure by empaquetage is shown in Pictures 75a, b, c.

We have dealt with the verification of the actual human figure. But what about its symbol? It is obvious that even plants and the most common objects remind us of the human figure. For example, when looking at a mushroom, a poppyhead, flowering garlic or corn, even an exclamation mark turned upside down or some letters. Children first regard a circle with 'two legs' as a human figure. Later they build their first plasticine people from two spheres one on top of the other, but even their thumb with its nail, the index finger on which they put their mother's thimble, or a wooden spoon, or sieve can turn into a human figure. I do not know whether the same thing is said in France, Germany or Australia as it is in Bohemia – a nail is hit on the *head* while pins are pulled out of material by the *head* and one slices *heads* of cabbage and lettuce.

77 *The White Lady* was made by tying layers of bits of soft paper with thread. The figure stands well on a wider base made of the edges of the crumpled paper. The head was shaped by crumpling the paper and the hands by twisting it.

78 *Mr Knot* is not just a poor fellow made from a handkerchief. If you look carefully you can see that he looks like a noble knight with his visor closed and plumes on his helmet. Even the shadow is noble and scarlet is the colour of kings. Let us imagine how simple and charming it would be to act a play with the knight and the White Lady just before the small children have to go to bed. A green scarf with three knots could play the terrible dragon.

79 *'Bighead'* recalls the huge figures on the Easter Islands. This one even has two interesting grooves. In one you can see a closed eye, in the other a mouth with a mysterious smile. At this point I would like to remind you now that a part of creative abilities is to know and also to 'feel' which ordinary stones can be placed side by side to create a tension of shapes (round–sharp–edged, large–small), contrast of colours (dark–light), contrast of surfaces (smooth–rough), contrast of lines (short–long, in various directions), etc.

79

In idiomatic language a Czech child has a head like an onion or a poppy-head, but also a head like a kohlrabi or a coconut. It only remains for me to point out that creative activity is always connected with creative observation. Both must constantly be brought to life, if only in something as simple as the careful arrangement of suitable stones side by side or the tying of a curious or unruly knot in a handkerchief.

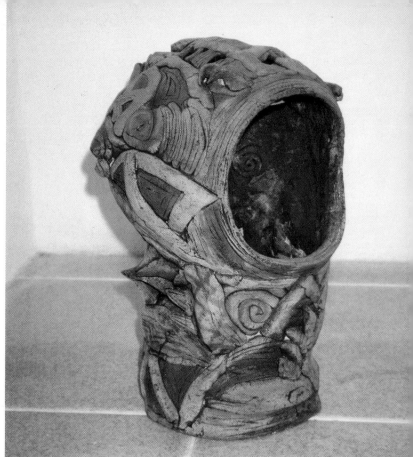

A

B

C

D

A *Olbram Zoubek* (born 1926), *Muse*, 1977, cement, height 2.2 m. A slender girl floats above the lawn in Vojan Park, Prague. The children think she is intently listening to silent music or verses.

B *Michal Jakeš* (born 1969), *Diver*, 1992, ceramic, height 50 cm. Children believe this to be an artistic impression of a diving helmet which is overgrown with aquatic plants because it has lain at the bottom of the sea for so long. It remains the sole witness of a tragedy, for the diver himself probably perished in the sea. (This is the work of a student at the Studio of ceramics and porcelain under Professor Václav Šerák at the University of Applied Arts, Prague.)

C *Matyáš Bernard Braun* (1684–1738), *Titans*, 1714, sandstone. In contrast to the other muses, neither of the muscle men – giants – can move. On their shoulders they are carrying the left side of the portal of the Clam-Galas Palace in Prague.

D For centuries these rocks have watched the Baltic Sea, keenly and motionless witnessing the constant struggle between the coastal cliffs and the predatory waves. Don't the rocks remind you of a human profile?

E *Jan Kment* (born 1961), *Stilt Walker*, 1992, plaster and wood, height 8 m. This fat white man on stilts also seems to be a muse, but rather that of a poet-humorist. Due to the fact that she cannot rise above her happy protégé because of her corpulence, the 'muse' has taken some stilts and cautiously observes her artist from a height. (This is the work of a student at the sculpture studio of Professor Kurt Gebauer, University of Applied Arts in Prague).

F A plaster replica (modification) of a Papuan dance mask from New Guinea preserves the original ornamental style of the eyes and nose. It portrays the supernatural being who protects fertility.

G *Jiří Sozanský* (born 1946), a detail of the painting *The Fall of the Angels*, 1991, 330 × 230 cm. The Czech artist has combined sculpture with painting bringing suggestive expression to his idea of the ancient myth of the struggle between heaven and hell – good and evil. Human legs and arms emerge from layers of writhing crushed pastel colours as though rising from water and fire.

E

F

G

4

Ordinary Things?

The transformation of things. No chair is the same. Assemblage – the strange meeting of objects. Pencils for a giant. Clocks to show spring. Children as designers. Cars, aeroplanes and other flying objects. Toys for the first-year pupils. Some still lifes with alarm clocks.

---

80 *The older children invented bright blocks* in various combinations for their younger brothers and sisters and for the first-year pupils in their school that were still playing with them. On each side of the block is a rebus. On the six sides of the blocks there are cats or clowns chasing each other. But they are always drawn over two or more sides. And so the children have to work hard to count how many figures there actually are on each block.

81 *How did I make a boat?* Well, of course, from a plastic coca-cola bottle which I could easily cut, coloured paper and paint. That's what one of the older boys would tell you, who did not need any instruction for his design. He worked everything out for himself. The bottom of the boat is weighted with plasticine to prevent it from capsising. Can you imagine an entire fleet on the fish pond?

From early on children make friends with objects. They look at them from all sides and wherever possible they look inside as well. Even when they know what the adults use the object for, nothing prevents them from using it for their own purposes when playing with it. Four-year-old children investigate patient grandmother's tempting box of buttons, beads, threads and balls of wool. They move into the lower accessible parts of the kitchen cupboard and try to find out how much a rolling pin, saucepan or small lid can stand. And if their father has garden tools or even a small workshop he knows that he will have no peace until he allots his small children some space for their activities.

When small children play, objects are transformed. You can build a house or a strange animal from a pot. A crystal vase turned upside down becomes an ice palace, a prison for the enchanted princess. A wonderful nest can be made from feather beds, but you can also 'fly' on them as if on a cloud. The easychair turned upside down is an excellent instrument panel for a pilot to which a few alarm clocks and a vacuum cleaner may be added so that the

82a

82b

aeroplane produces the correct noises. And how lucky those children are, whose parents are always willing to fall in with their games. When these children are about 10 years old their art teachers can distinguish them from other children who were subdued by adults by being, so to say, permanently tidied away in front of the television, where they stared at everything and anything with a bored expression.

It seems that the 10-year-old remembers in creative work games with everyday objects from preschool days. So let's talk with the children about an ordinary chair. We had a chair from school at our disposal, but we could equally find lots of interesting things to say about the adventures of an old armchair or a kitchen chair. How much benefit we have had from various types of chairs! Let's imagine a situation in which the chairs that we take for granted were to disappear. We would have to stand through a theatre performance and probably miss a lot. The dentist would have to lie us flat on the floor or prop us up against a wall to fill a tooth. Are we even able to enumerate all the various types of this irreplaceable piece of furniture? Let's try it with the children. Do they know them all? What do they look like – a chair, a highchair, a footstool, an easychair, a pew, a workbench, a deckchair, a milking stool, a sofa-bed, a bathchair, a wheelchair, a couch, an armchair, a hassock, an ottoman, a dentist's chair, a garden chair, a rocking chair, a seat. Just think how funny it would be if we were to try and use an armchair for milking or gave a workbench to an executive in an office.

But let's return to our 'school chair'. Could somebody add up how many

82a *The seat for Pythagoras* is regularly and symmetrically finished off with red threads and paper triangles. The shape of the chair itself allowed for a geometric solution. The older children who made it already knew something of the Pythagoras theorem (i.e. that the square on the hypotenuse of a rightangled triangle is equal to the sum of squares on the other two sides). They were quite definite that it was a chair for an architect or a mathematician. The photograph shows that the seat for Pythagoras can also fly. It hangs on the wall on a strong hook, making the children aware of creative work as a process in which several variations offer innumerable possibilities of solution.

82b *The chair for spinning dreams* is finished off with lint from coloured threads and seems to form the contrast to the logical strictness of the preceding chair, laughing heartily at everything serious or methodical. And the dreams you would dream sitting in it would be very happy and fantastic.

82c *This chair – a beauty –* is draped with coloured strips as if it were trying out materials from which it would like to have its clothes made. In the end it puts them all on.

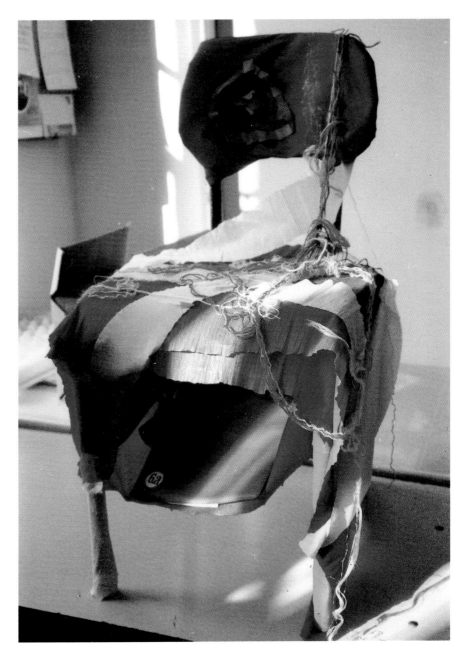

82c

hours we sit on one of them in the course of the school year? And how many hours such a chair 'works' in ten years? Our chair listens silently and with concentration in school, day after day, year in, year out. It must have heard the same things many times, and so it knows geography and natural science probably better than the pupil fidgeting on it and regarding it more like an instrument of torture. It could also provide a wonderful means of transport into regions and events described by the teacher, or into book or film.

Perhaps chairs have their secret nature, their secret preferences. Let's try to make them visible by the creative means at our disposal. In large boxes prepare various types of material ready for the children to choose from. They

83a

83b

can 'dress up' their chair with coloured papers, bits of material, netting and ribbons. Long, thin wooden or metal strips can give the chair a new shape, fix wings to the arm and back rests. We can wrap coloured thread, string and ribbons round the chair like cobwebs. We are not afraid to dress it up in an interesting manner, perhaps in an anorak or jumper that we have stuffed a little. From our clothes it will appear at first glance that the chair belongs only to us, like a faithful animal with odd corners, wings and snout. It is also important to discuss the name of the chair, what it can do, what adventures you can dream up for it. What does its owner look like? Is it the chair for Punch, for a sorcerer, a water nymph, a mathematician or entomologist? And when the children 'undress' the chair again so that they have something to sit on, when all the chairs look so much alike, the children feel sorry.

But there also exist things that have a special effect on us because of their unchanged appearance. Doesn't your house have some happy and some sad 'eyes', if we compare eyes and windows? Perhaps an old typewriter has become an honourable and interesting sculpture, whether it reminds you of an ogre with long teeth or not. The mop (see Picture 83b) does not have to be shaped into some sort of puppet because if you have once held it in your arms you know that it is pleasant to the touch. It behaves like a creature by its appearance alone, or rather like a shaggy, elongated, trusting, long-haired dog, and you don't know at first which is its head or its tail.

83a *A devil – or an infernal machine?* Neither the one nor the other. This is an old typewriter that attracted two small children like a magnet with its mysterious keys and levers. In the end it got a yellow nose made from a stapler and buttons for eyes. But even without the nose and eyes it would remain a devil for the children.

83b *Grandpa Know-all* is the class mascot. He was also made by transforming ordinary objects – a broom to which a few bits were added, beads from an abacus, stuffed socks and an old lampshade. (His full name is Grandpa-Know-all Tell-all). It seems that the puppeteer, the creator of animated films, sees and thinks in the same way as children.

84a *Small beetles and their mother.* Similar sculptures with transferred meaning are created in the precious moments of 'spring cleaning', when the children are over-eager to help you only because they discover lots and lots of mysterious and beautiful things that are first sorted in various heaps and only then put away in their proper place or discarded. Just see what arose by sheer chance from some useless little bottles! 'Mummy' has the typical beetle eyes on the side of her head. That gave rise to the name. Anyway, have you ever seen a little family dressed in these black-and-white stripes? They could not be anything except beetles.

84a

84b   84c

84b *The horned animal* was made from a rubber bell into which a boy put a horseshoe and then added beads from an abacus. After the photograph was taken the horned animal was dismantled and everything tidied away.

84c *The foreman.* The children produced several variations by heaping things on top of each other. This seemed to them the best. Foremen look after the tools and keep an eye on the apprentices in the workshop. They wear flat caps, and have a severe look in their bulging eyes, and a long moustache so that the apprentices are afraid of them. The foreman also had to be dismantled and tidied away. Free assemblage is, rather, a free manipulation of objects and the choosing of the most successful variation. The children had no intention of fixing anything firmly with nails or glue.

85

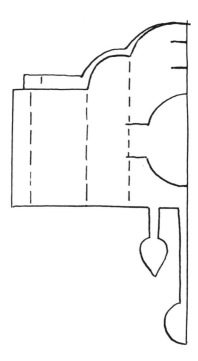

Creative artists also feel an intimate relationship with some objects. One of the most interesting and earliest of the 'important' objects was the *Bottle Drier* exhibited in 1914 by Marcel Duchamp. It is a cylindrical object in five sections with spikes on each rim. It reminded the children of a five-layered cake with candles. You can think of it as you will, but it is best as what it is, a bottle drier. Marcel Duchamp chose it as such as an object with an aesthetic function. If you want to see a reproduction of this extraordinary drier, you will find it in Norbert Lypton's book *Landmarks of the World of Art: The Modern World* in the chapter dealing with Dadaism, Surrealism, New Realism and Pop-Art. When years ago there was a Duchamp exhibition in Prague, the children went to 'have a look at Paris' by inspecting with an amused grin on their faces an empty sealed glass vessel with the caption that it contained pure, unadulterated Paris air. You probably also know people who bring home pebbles, little flasks containing water from various seas or sand from beach or desert as decoration or souvenirs from their journeys. Many years ago the children from one class gave me a huge, blown up rubber toy as a goodbye present – a giraffe. For some reason it has retained to this day the breath they expended to blow it up. And this ordinary toy became for me something that was of greater value than any other present.

86a *A clock showing spring.* Smaller children folded sheets of stiff paper in half and sketched their design of a clock (see diagram). Then they cut it out, folded it over as if making a box and pressed the dial inwards. When they had decided on the shape of the clock they flattened it out again and drew the design. It was their job to express in colour what time the clock preferred to show. Note that the colours are cold at the bottom and change into warmer lighter shades as is the case with the advance of spring.

86b *A clock for Grandmother's birthday present.* The small designer made it rather high, with sombre colours and black-and-white stripes at all the edges. Instead of the door for the cuckoo to appear he put a red heart which he thought suitable for a proper greeting.

We constantly say that there is no such thing as an 'ordinary object'. Everything lies in the eye of the beholder. The Czech writer Karel Čapek wrote a short story *The Inventor with a Rare Verbal Sense of Humour*. This inventor first of all looked for the words and then he created his invention accordingly.

The place for waiting is the waiting room, why then should we not have a place for being bored – the boring room, with many instruments – bores? What the literati think up the children prefer to produce more concretely, even inventions not mentioned in the story. How would you invent a spoon for slow eaters, spectacles for seeing everything happy and rose-coloured, a round-the-corner-looking telescope, a noise-maker?

Perhaps it has just occurred to you that these 'inventions' are quite as important for our civilised world as real inventions, that kind humour and amused laughter is healthy and improves relationships between people. And perhaps you have also found out that our civilisation in all seriousness produces many senseless things that are hardly a laughing matter. Think what damage can be caused by a hand grenade or other 'clever' inventions whose only purpose is to kill!

However, there are other modest little inventions which mankind hands down from generation to generation, perfecting only the shape because they

87a

87a, b, c *Let me present a designer* who, without the aid of models, thought out his car first in a plane made up of three connected parts (ground plan and two side views). He then cut out the whole shape and hey presto, he had his car. How would you start? With the side view to which you would add a wide strip – the view of the car from above, from in front and from the back. For the less skilful, a piece of advice: draw the car from the side on a separate piece of paper and cut it out. This unattached side view can easily be traced: we need it twice. It is also useful for checking the width of the glass and the parts of the bonnet from above, on the ground plan of the car. Don't forget to allow for overlapping the paper on the top strip, so that you can glue the parts together. And only then start thinking of how to make the wheels. The boy constructed them separately on wooden spills (see diagram). Note that the colour strips of the decoration follow the natural shape of the car.

realise that they will never produce anything more ingenious. It would be worthwhile to erect a monument to their creators or inventors. The children tried to express their admiration for the perfection of the invention of an ordinary pencil or a clock (see Pictures 85 and 86). They constructed huge musical instruments from paper in the same way. At one time we had fantastically shaped violins and guitars hanging on the walls of the music room. They were not mechanical imitations, the children tried to improve on the shapes, and brought

87b

87c

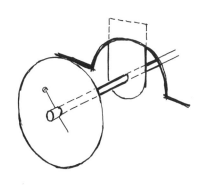

from home various strange horns, small drums and rattles, instruments they had thought up themselves.

Children also successfully magnified ('monumentalised') various small objects, as if they were intended for a giant or as if Gulliver had lost them. From various boxes, wrappings, gummed-paper and the cardboard cylinders round which carpets are rolled, 2-metre long keys on a huge key ring can be made. You could hang them near the school gates, a suitable place for a monument to this clever invention. A huge mug and plate with a bun made from painted paper could stand in the grass. If you crumble a roll over the bun it will suddenly seem to have become real for our small feathered friends gathering round. In the same way Gulliver might have lost his pocket watch, a toothbrush and toothpaste.

From their earliest age we educate children to admire speed. Tiny children have become so used to the cars in the town that they greet them from afar and for a time they form a huge world for them. They pretend to be cars or aeroplanes and it is enough if they make the necessary noise, spread their arms wide like wings and tirelessly run along the pavement. But subconsciously we may feel what the Canadian theoretician on media, Marshall McLuhan (1911–1980) wrote in his book *How to Understand Media* in the chapter 'The Bicycle, Motorbike and Aeroplane' and in the chapter 'The Car: a Mechanical Bride'.

Here are a few quotes referring to the car:
'If all the rhinoceroses and hippopotamuses of the world were to come

88a

88a, b *The girls produced a car* as part of the attractions on a merry-go-round or in a haunted castle. This is a box pasted over with paper and then painted in colours so bright that it clearly belongs to a fairground.

together in one city, they could not create such a threat and explosive intensity as we experience every day from the combustion engine...'

'...Will the car survive? It is odd that in this fast progressing age where constant change has become the only constant in our life we never ask this question. Of course the answer will be negative. In the age of electricity the wheel itself will become outmoded. People at the heart of the automobile industry realise that the car is a temporary phenomenon...'

'...The car gave the democratic knight simultaneously a horse, weapons and tremendous impudence, and thus transformed him into a badly guided missile...'

'...The car is the perfect demonstration of uniform standardised mecha-

88b

Enjoy comparing the real dashboard of an old Aero car (so called 'Tingaling Aero') with the dashboard made by a small boy for his 'garden' car.

88c *A land rover* for travels through the African bush was produced by the clever hands of two girl designers. The car is comfortable, has a movable roof and the doors can be opened. It has a lot of room for luggage and is called Mr. Mopedshee. It is the small brother of the car owned by the Adamsons, wellknown from their African nature films.

nism ... it has transformed all space that joins or separates people...' (i.e. town and country, communication systems, etc.).

People seem not only to gain pleasure, but also fear from the things that they invent. The inventions often suddenly turn on the inventor. This fear is age-old. It survives in the legends of the Kichu tribe. The story tells of the rebellion of objects against man for all his insensitive handling. The pots boiled their inventor after he was killed by the hens and ground by the mills. This legend seems to develop the thought expressed by an ancient painting on a vase by a Peruvian artist from the early culture of the Chimor (1st–6th century BC, preceding the culture of the Incas). The painting depicts animated cudgels and other weapons rebelling against man. Comparing the old legends with McLuhan's writing we realise that they were not written as fairytales for children. Children of today already play with cars, digital toys, they handle videos, television and computers. They play with numerous variations of automobiles which they can draw accurately, even though we may feel some 'educational' doubts. Is it the fault of the car that it has become a blessing or a curse? Should we persuade the children to walk rather than drive? Or to influence them in their drawing lessons to draw their cars with electric drive, natural gas or solar batteries? Children will only answer that something like that is already under the bonnet of their car. The ability to design, which we are trying to develop in the children by the use of simple topics, also means encouraging good spatial imagination, so that when the children, as adult engineers, are introduced to the computer which in front of their eyes produces the construction of a house, chair, car or aeroplane, they will be sorry that they cannot touch the shape. The hands, of such basic importance in the devel-

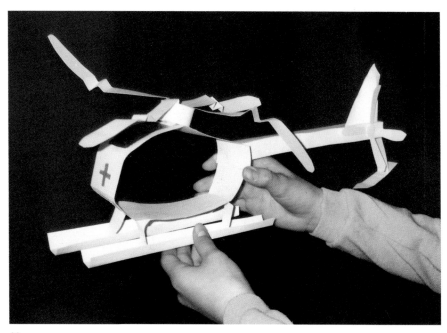

89

89

The helicopter ambulance for badly accessible terrain is the work of a small designer with particularly good spatial imagination. Children rarely design so that the view from the side is incomplete. The boy judged that the most typical view of a helicopter is from below or above. He was right, because the rotor blades are difficult to see from the side. The runners recall a hydroplane.

opment of man, will be condemned to a mere turning and pushing of buttons. As if it were not enough that the screen has already excluded taste and smell from the human senses!

When looking through the pictures showing how the children manage in their own way to design a vehicle we realise that they are interested not only in the external shape and surface, but also in the possible construction of a 'technical organism', which by no means accidentally resembles the

90

90 *A balloon* must be included among the flying machines. The girl solved the net for the balloon, which can be inserted into the paper 'cage' and blown up. The gondola shaped like a small boat is solved in an original way. The crew need not fear being shipwrecked.

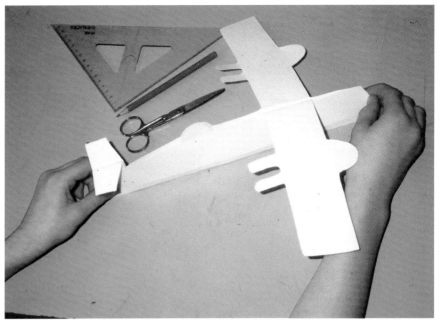

91a *The aeroplane* is symmetrical along its axis and can be easily · mistaken for a bird. The simple construction of birds with spread wings helped the children also in the construction of simple aeroplanes (see page 46). All aeroplanes up to page 97 are based on it, each is an original without working instructions or a plan for the children to follow, or the use of a building set.

symmetrical outer skeleton of a beetle or the carapace of a turtle, the aerodynamic shape of a dolphin or a flying swan. It seems as if we have foilowed the same thought process since the times when early man tried to protect his body and head with a primitive leather helmet and wooden shield, screen, cave or shelter. The car, aeroplane or ship is still the magnified outer clothing, armour or shell for the defenceless easily injured animal that man basically is. Means of transport satisfy the ancient longing for fast and safe travel. That they are not the fastest or safest is obvious to everybody. Humans came to terms with their envy of the creatures and the natural elements that can travel

91b

91b *Before the children start the construction of an aeroplane* they must have a good idea of the ratio of the wings and body. On a folded piece of paper the children drew this with the aid of a ruler. They also worked out details that could be cut out straight away from the folded paper, such as the place for the fuel tanks, the flaps for the front edges of the wings, where the propellers might be fixed, the cabin for the pilot, etc. Note that the aeroplane is broad when seen from below. The red stripe is the flat 'belly' of the plane, where the designer will add the undercarriage and wheels. The children can paste coloured paper to the plane or use paints.

92a

92a *In this training plane* by a very small designer the experienced instructor sits at the back above the rudder. The pilot under instruction sits in the centre of the plane. The little figures can be inserted between the several parts of the body and glued together. The wings are fringed, recalling birds and butterflies with their broad shape; this is why they are stiffened crossways with spills. The designer admitted that this might also be an improved pedalo, a pedal boat.

so much more efficiently, when they first mounted a horse or travelled down river on the first primitive raft. Now people are so obsessed by speed that they sit down in front of the television screen, push a few buttons and via the satellite find out what the fruit harvest was like in the Antipodes and immediately afterwards check what the astronauts had for lunch. It is not surprising that children draw a car far more realistically than an animal or a plant, for we

92b

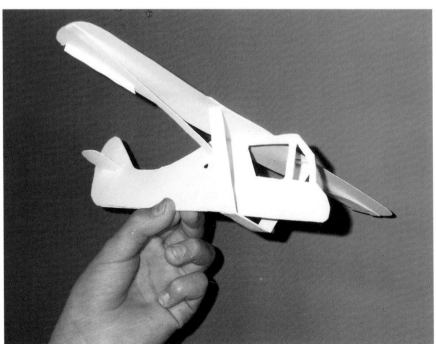

92b *This glider* is an example of a faultless technical construction with clear spatial conception. The long wings are strengthened with two different braces. The wider ones are also the undercarriage on which the glider rolls along the grass.

93 *Hydroplane 'Mouse'.* An older
boy started out by considering two
pairs of wings. If a biplane can have
two wings one above the other, then
why should it not be possible to place
the smaller wings in front of the
larger. And this is how the ears
appeared. The pointed nose of
a mouse also fitted into the construction. Since the plane was really very
successful, the designer considered
a stand on which he could
demonstrate it. This is how the
runners and the definitive design were
decided on. The plane can land on
snow or water. The black 'eyes' are
the windows of the pilot's cabin. This
technical shape clearly belongs with
the aeroplanes in this chapter and not
among the animals in Chapter 3.

replaced real animals with simplified animal toys they can touch and schema-
tised animal heroes from cartoons and films.

So we should not be surprised by the design ability of a boy (Pictures
87a, b, c) who without any problem in a flat drawing almost immediately
guessed what the complicated bodywork of a car would look like in space. I
would like to convince you, with the aid of a large number of illustrations, that
during their artistic education children do not need design instructions or
predrawn plans from which they cut out parts to create an aeroplane.

We are concerned with creative education and not the construction of
model aeroplanes. The children know much better than many adults the typical
shape of an aeroplane or a car. For a plane to remain a plane a certain ratio
must be preserved between its three parts (body, wings, rudder). The children
seldom make a mistake and immediately realise that their design looks more
like a flying goose. Boys and girls are sure in their work although older girls
show a somewhat greater interest in the romanticism of forms in their choice
of shapes. They usually prefer the design of a historic vehicle or an electric
car travelling along a mountain track to an enchanted castle and they decorate it suitably.

The children are also capable designers of amphibious vehicles. On dry

94a

94a *This observation plane* shows how smaller children design, who long for the technical appearance of the aeroplane but cannot help showing little figures as well. Note how the colour solution contrasts with that of 'The humming bird'.

land wheels or runners emerge, in the water they push out a screw for a motor, which in the air is exchanged for aerofoils like a helicopter's. Thanks to books, films and cartoons the children can also create UFOs. Rockets are discussed in Chapter 5, where I have included them as examples of technical structures similar to spires, transmitters and observation towers.

The children are sometimes sorry that their paper mobiles do not move. Their toys have a key or a mechanical spiral, a perpetuum mobile or they can use a battery. But I can make some suggestions here. The simplest mobile

94b

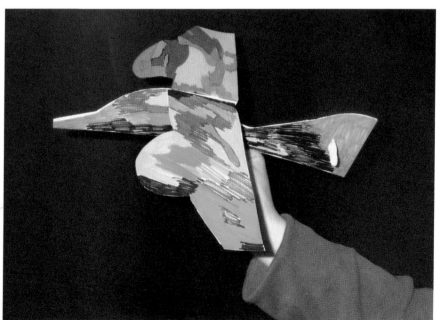

94b *'The humming bird'.* This small plane got its name from its colours. The humming bird's motley colouring is its camouflage. After landing, this small plane also merges into the background. It has a long 'beak' to help it cut through the air – the humming bird has a long beak to suck nectar from flowers.

94c *This biplane* was constructed by an 11-year-old boy with good designing ability. From the beginning his spatial conception was accurate. He cut the wings twice. Before he finally glued all the parts together with their braces he added bright colours that are well suited to the shape of the plane.

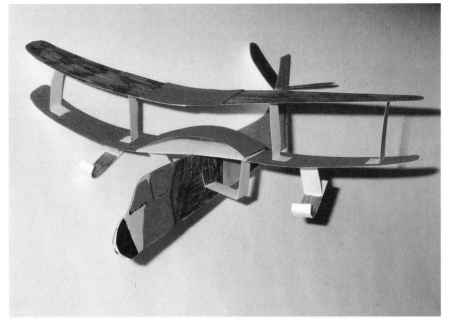

94c

to be controlled by childish hands is the paper windmill or a sail. The children will be able to fit it to a fantastic car – a light paper sculpture they have created. The car could move by itself on an asphalt or concrete surface. Before the children begin, describe to them what the experiments of the most ancient inventors might have looked like and suggest that they try to construct their mobile vehicles in a similar way. Records exist of ancient carts with sails attached and driven by the wind. People in China thought these up a long time ago. These sailing carts were driven over plains and even measured

94d

94d *This propeller-driven aeroplane* is reminiscent of a good-natured bumblebee, more a toy for small children who accept that the fast rotation of the propeller can be simulated by painting it with spirals.

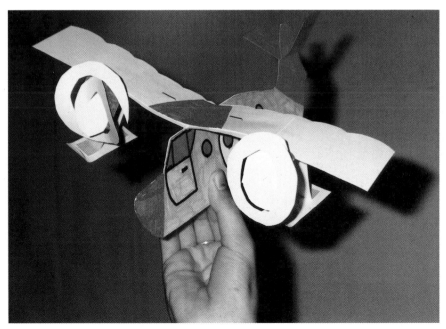

95a

95a *The prisms with four small animals* are made up of two paper cubes, each produced by folding a strip (see diagram). In the upper squares are the animals' heads, in the lower the bodies. The whole animal has the same colouring. If this is dark, then the background should be light to make the animal stand out more. Their tamers, the clowns, got in amongst them.

distances for the cartographers. The Dutch mathematician Simon Stevin at the beginning of the seventeenth century invented a narrow carriage on wheels with space for forty passengers that was fitted with sails and could reach a speed of 40 kilometres an hour.

What today would seem like a pleasant little child's toy was a serious step forward in developing science. As further motivation I recommend the book *The Ascent of Man* by the mathematician and author of popular BBC science programs, Jacob Bronowski (London, 1973).

95b

95b *The heads and bodies of the animals* were interchanged by simply turning the paper cubes. These are threaded onto a rolled paper cylinder sufficiently elastic to hold the cubes in place. A play wall for small children may be erected from these movable cubes. Each side of the mobile toys was made by one child, eighteen in all participated.

98

96a, b *How many cats and mice are chasing each other* on the block? The first-year pupils have to find out. The toys were made for them by their third-year playmates. These two photographs show one cube, on which a boy placed a cat so that its body or at least its tail reached as many sides as possible. The black background is artistically suitable for the coloured cat, and in any case, cats like the dark.

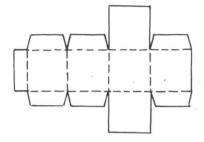

96a, b

96c

96c *The juggling clowns* chase each other over the cubes like the cats. The small children must count them and also find out how many balls the clowns are juggling with. That is not an easy task when you are faced with six sides to a cube.

99

97

97 *A bagful of fleas* and a bagful of misery – these were the ridiculous sculptures on the lawn in front of our school. Two of the younger boys were hard at work painting the entire shape to indicate what was hidden inside – fidgety fleas and weeping misery.

It may have occurred to you that all the cars, planes and ships described in these pages could be toys. It is indeed artists who design toys, and it is studied as a discipline at art colleges. Their favourite materials were and are textiles, wood and paper. It used to be the custom in former Czechoslovakia that mothers or grandmothers sewed the dolls and their clothes for their daughters or granddaughters, while grandfathers cut puppets from wood, as well as horses and carts and a whole series of small animals. Every father ought to be able to cut a whistle or properly glue a kite together. It is said that in

98a

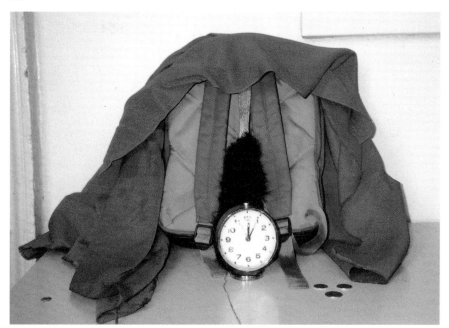

98a *Waiting for the day trip to begin.* This is the most suitable title for the still life with alarm clock produced by two boys. They were given several objects to choose from and selected a rucksack and a piece of red material. The shapes of the still life are quiet, composed along the axis. The tension is only caused by the contrasting colours of red against light and dark green. The white dial of the alarm clock produces an expressive light effect. Time plays an important part in every waiting, always causing tension.

98b *We are back from our trip.*
Several boys produced this interesting still life. The arrangement of the objects could not have arisen arbitrarily. It contains thought, composition, adjustment. Light areas alternate with dark. Two different shades of red are used purposely and do not seem to clash. Neglected boots 'walk' all over the still life, obviously tired after the excursion, just like their owners. The whole is again dominated by the alarm clock which measured the time of the trip and is now resting under a grey cloth.

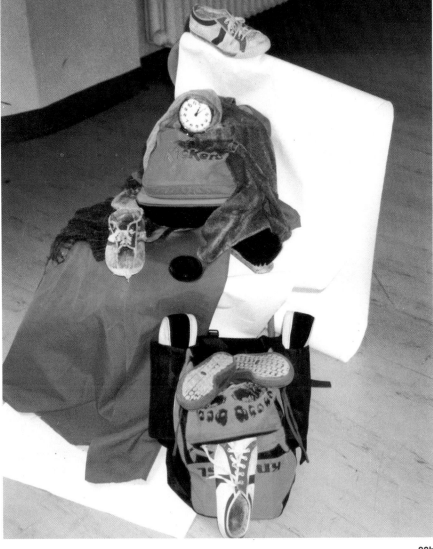

98b

'The End of the Tennis Shoes'. This still life proves that the life span meted out to the tennis shoes is gone for ever. Even these objects which will sooner rather than later be thrown into the garbage bin, are surprisingly pleasant to look at since they are marked by the traces of boyish games and amusements and bear witness to a period in the life of their owner.

Japan the older sisters sew dolls for the younger ones. In our school it is the custom to make presents for the first-year pupils coming up. These are blocks and figurines (see Pictures 96a, b), they could also be aeroplanes or small cars. Every small, independent creative work should be fun, full of kind humour and have something to say to the younger sibling or friend.

I have left our poetical meeting with objects to the end. This is not assemblage in the proper meaning of the word. A still life with an alarm clock, that is a 'meeting of object with time' always has something to say to us. There are clocks of happiness, clocks of tension, minutes of terror. We can create different environments for the actual alarm clock as the symbol of time lived through in various ways. By strewing things about the children can express hurry, impatience; by things tidily arranged, on the other hand, a long period of waiting as if standing in a queue until we are called. Children prefer to arrange the still lifes themselves before drawing or painting them.

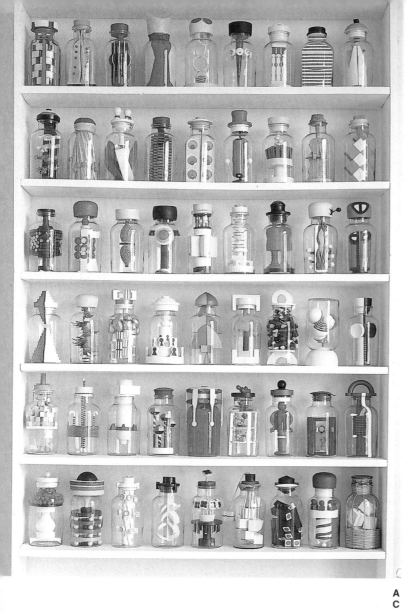

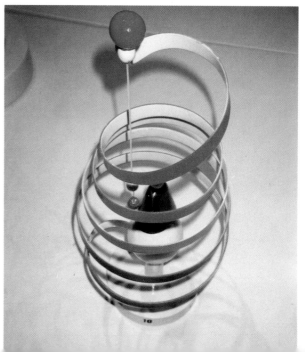

A *Vladimír Preclík* (born 1929), *54 weeks of a good year*, 1975, glass, painted and gilt wood, 3 m. Do you know that sailors, while away long hours, used to construct miniature ships inside bottles? This artist placed one small piece of sculptured art, one of his small joys, into a bottle each week.

B *Vladimír Syrovátka* (born 1938), *Hour-glass*, from the cycle *Tribute to Man Ray*, 1989, height 32 cm. Do you believe this is the first invention to stop time? If you turn the hour-glass upside down, you can enjoy Christmas for as long as you wish.

C *Vratislav K. Novák* (born 1942), *Cyclot Fly*, 1987–88, steel, brass and PVC, $25 \times 20 \times 20$ cm. A mobile recalls how, since time immemorial, man has regretted that Nature has not endowed him with wings. Hence, he has fantasies and creates ingenious technical structures.

D *Svatopluk Král* (born 1926), *Jumping spring*, 1987, painted steel, wood, height 70 cm. Many ringing, tinkling mobile sculptures by this Czech artist awaited for children's hands at an exhibition to set them in motion and let them resound. They are also artistically and technically perfected machines often used in rehabilitation work.

E *Vladimír Rocman* (born 1929), *Little Martin the Martian*, a mobile cut-out for children, 1989, paper, sticks, thread, height 80 cm. When children cut out the parts of the small Martian, stick them together and assemble according to the instructions, the robot can walk on its own on a leaning surface thanks to a balance beam.

F Old folk toys, carved from wood, can move too. The dolls have an opening in the back and a string. Pull it and the first doll begins to rock her baby and the second beat the butter.

G *Vladimír Syrovátka* (born 1938), *Spectacles*, 1985. This witty creation is a wonderful invention perhaps for inquisitive children who want to look through a key-hole into a forbidden room.

H *Vladimír Syrovátka, Summer skates*, 1985. Children would love to invent fantastic shoes, e.g. slippers on wheels, fisherman's wellingtons with flippers, jumping boots made from the springs of a couch.

E   F

G

H

5

People's Homes

Building does not only mean putting one brick next to another, a house next to a house. You find the material and you build a house. Tents and other types of shelter. Constructions rising from the surface of one sheet of paper. Climbing frames and slides. Towers.

99 *This construction was formed by arranging coloured clothes pegs.* The children kept to the perpendicular and vertical directions. The structure gives the impression of a beautiful machine. Its structural element, the clothes pegs, is not covered by any façade. The building is a rather spacious scaffolding.

100 *We are building a town* – the work of several small children. Each of them had to draw a part of a street consisting of several houses to form a harmonious whole in shape and colour. The children cut out the houses, bent them along the edges and cut out parts for the windows and doors to give them a three-dimensional effect. Then they started to make up the collage working from the top of the panel down. The houses that the children placed side by side again formed streets matching in shape and colour to produce a pleasant and gay view of a town.

'...man would not have built anything at all, if children had not learned to build when playing. The Parthenon and the Taj Mahal start in play, the cupola in the Sultan's Palace and Watt Tower and Machu-Picchu...' writes Jacob Bronowski in the *Ascent of Man*. In the Chapter entitled 'Long Childhood' he considers the uniqueness of man... 'Art and science equally prove the tremendous malleability of human thought...'

If we were ants we would have erected an ant hill during the Gothic period in the same way as at the end of the twentieth century. The swallows, too, build their nests now as they did then. But we are human beings and from generation to generation we think up and improve various types of shelter and buildings for widely varying purposes. Let us consider what we can take over from older generations, what we can learn from nature and how to make use of new materials.

Pictures 99, 100 demonstrate that the construction of an unusual house is like the construction of a whole town. In the same way we cannot be satis-

101

101 *A small girl made this moss house* over the weekend. It is a model of the first purpose-built house, a sort of screen of twigs and pieces of bark. Primitive people covered their shelters with reeds or grasses. The girl used a cushion of moss and leaves. Covering houses with beautiful turf also appears in contemporary architecture.

fied with the elemental, chaotic and inconsiderate extension or destruction of part of a house, or the extension or destruction of part of a town. If we speak of architecture we think of the art of building constructions that fulfil two functions: useful and aesthetic. In the wider sense of the word architecture means the creation of man's entire environment. We then speak of the architecture of a region, towns, parts of towns. This is how a dictionary would explain architecture to children, but what do 10-year-olds understand of these terms? They come across 'houses' every day, and they no longer even notice them. Let's try to make them aware of houses in playing a game. How has the architect provided for them, where has he or she put our house in the street? Let's see how the sun moves along the street, which windows face the sun when it rises,

102

102 *A house made of thistles* is a structured model of an interesting spherical shape.

103

104

103 *The melon house* gets its round shape from nature. The structure is modelled on a loaf of bread in soft aluminium foil. The roof contains instruments, radar, aerials and solar panels for heating purposes. The house can also serve as shelter for astronauts on the moon.

104 *My home – my castle.* The boy used folded sheet metal and cut doors into it with plumber's cutters. The details on the top are soldered on. In reality the architect would build such a structure from concrete. The effect of the structure is monumental and impregnable.

when it sets. Which windows do the rays peep into during the day? Are there windows that the architect and the sun thought least of?

Observing some house we declare that its facade is perfect, like a statue, and by that we mean that its facade is perfectly arranged. No architect thinks that he or she has designed a displeasing house. Let us give the quality of a house various marks as if in school. Which of the five houses closest to where you live would get excellent? Can you say why? But first you must walk round them and look at them from a distance. If you can, have a look at least at the staircase leading to the upper floors, only then will you do justice to its qualities. If they could walk round it, would the children be able to draw its ground plan? Could they say why it would be nice to live in? If you live in a completely built-up street, it is also possible to choose the most attractive among those houses close by and to imagine how nice it would be to live on the second floor with the beautiful balcony.

Children from high-rise blocks of flats will be a little unsure, perhaps. We can reassure them that today architects are doing their best to find some ways of making these large, monotonous blocks come to life, so that they do not resemble crossroads with regular networks of windows. Some of the 'high-rise dwellers' may only have a kind thought for these windows when the setting sun is reflected in them and they glisten in all colours of the rainbow. But the architects probably did not take that into consideration at all and the children might all be asleep by that time. It is somewhat discouraging when a few horizontal and vertical lines across the whole sheet of paper are enough for a child to draw a house.

Let us not degrade contemporary architecture to settlements of 'miracles of boredom', let us discuss with the children what is new in the various architectural streams of the twentieth century. Working backwards we might reach the historical styles. At the beginning of our joint considerations of contemporary architecture we shall set a task for the children motivated by discussion. Imagine that you are part of a mature civilisation from another planet

105a

105b

105a *Pyramid.* The children tried to find out how many sticks from their bundle they could prop up against each other. Their task was to place as many as possible into the construction of the pyramid. They used a smaller pyramid inside, fixing the sticks in plasticine. But is has nothing in common with an Indian tepee. The Indians first of all erected a tripod tied together at the top. Then they leant further posts against the three main ones. The children like to try this in the open air.

105b *How do you put up a tent in the kitchen?* The children tried it with two inflatable li-los which they threw over two chairs placed back to back. The children can make an excellent tent palace if you lend them a large bedspread or curtain. They can throw it over a table and several chairs.

and that you have just landed on earth. Basically you are wise beings like humans, only you are small, about 5 cm high or even smaller. Immediately on landing you must solve the task of erecting a dwelling, a group of shelters for several families. What building material you use depends on the place where you land, in a forest, on the boundary of a field, on the outskirts of a town, on a building site or perhaps even on the balcony of some human dwelling. Have a good look round and choose a building material that is homogeneous so that your building can be erected and then extended. Don't forget that you are technically mature, as well as aesthetically feeling creatures from another planet, so you will not construct a heap of leaves or a cupboard with drawers of equal size.

The children usually complete their task in about a week. Collect their structures possibly accompanied by a written explanation from the builders

105c

105c

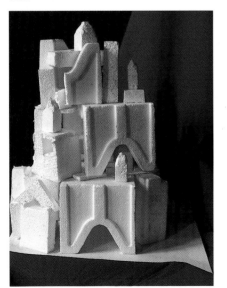

105c *Pyramid* – an arrangement of building elements, the higher it is, the wider its base. A small child had a quantity of variously shaped scraps of polystyrene, obtained by cutting up the packaging from electrical goods. By trial and error the most effective and firmest spot in the structure had to be found for each part. The pieces were glued together, and could also be quickly fastened with pins.

105d *A pyramid or a castle with two towers?* The children glued corks together. Small pieces of plasticine could also be used as a temporary binder.

108

106a *A tent – 'Striped Elephant'.* Two small children erected this unusual tent as protection against the burning summer sun and as their home. They threw a large striped blanket over a garden umbrella. The tent changed its shape according to how the children placed a deckchair and chair inside, to which they tied the corners of the blanket.

Basic types of hunters' and shepherds' tents:

 North Asiatic tribes and North American Indians

 Lapps

 Eskimos

 Palaeo-Asian tribes

Asian nomadic tribes, yurt

 Tibetan and Arab cattle breeders

 Tribes from Somalia and the neighbourhood of Lake Chad

 Patagonians and Araucanians

106a

and exhibit them in a suitable spot. The following examples show what material the children used for their buildings and will let you assess their structural approach. There was a very interesting spherical shape of about 50 cm in diameter made up of thistle heads which could be arranged as required and formed hollow spaces where the thistles adhered to each other (see Picture 102). The children made other structures from the green shells of conkers and spiral-shaped mounting 'tunnel flats' of eggshells threaded on wire. There were some constructions in cork (Picture 105d). There was one shape like

106b

106b *The interior of the tent* could change its purpose, 'the furniture' could be shifted so that the arrangement of the benches turned into a shop with a counter, a hospital and also a home for Indians who stored their catch and their furs in it. Once it even became a circus tent, where a plush bear and a rubber dog performed.

107a

107a *Smaller children invented
a slide* for a children's playground or
swimming pool. They had to produce
a spatial structure covering a stiff
sheet of paper. First they drew stripes
in spirals, cut them out and then
pulled them apart. Here the designers
tried to make stairs from parts of the
spirals.

a melon or a round bread loaf that was covered with aluminium foil with built-
in solar panels (Picture 103). A high building like a sky scraper was constructed
from a long soft metal strip and contained spherical shapes made of small
balls. There was a beautiful building made from coloured clothes pegs (Picture
99); then one made from polystyrene remnants recalling a termites' nest or
a strange pyramid (Picture 105c). One of the boys found an interestingly bent
piece of zinc sheet metal, modelled an entrance and soldered aerials to it. He
assured us that there was perfect air-conditioning inside (Picture 104). Our

107b

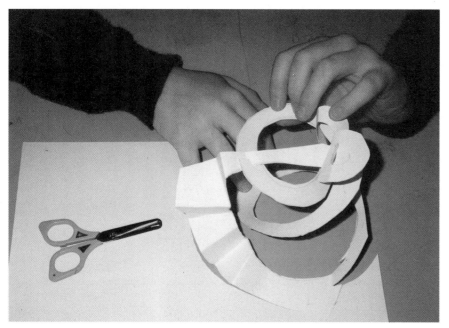

107b *In the next stage of design for
the slide* the boy tried to find
a support for the spiral. The children
could use sticks (drinking straws),
which they stuck into small clumps of
plasticine. Some children made the
entire structure of the slide and
climbing frames from stiff paper only.

110

108 *The slide for the swimming pool* is finished but this design differs from the previous illustrations. The simpler solution was creatively more effective because of its clarity, and with only one height dominant. The boy also suggested small figures of the correct size that would be able to use the slide.

attention was drawn to a secret spherical shape of opalescent glass, consisting of a lampshade to which coloured plasticine had been added, and into which the author had inserted coloured bits of felt-tipped pens, small lids and clothes pegs. A high boot had been interestingly transformed into a 'hotel' with the aid of paper windows glued to it. One of the small architects poured plaster of Paris into halved tennis balls and joined them into one white whole. They reminded us of an Eskimo igloo. The most frequent ideas were various composition from paper boxes, wrappings and wooden storage trays for fruit.

But the most important feature of the whole affair was the lively discussion which followed. First of all the children set aside those creations that in their composition and use of material recalled engines – technical architecture. The most technical impression was given by the clothes peg structure. This led us on to information on contemporary 'high-tech' architecture, which has the effect of a beautiful engine and where the architect does not hide any

109a

109a *This fantastic shape* on a children's playground was painted – here in cool colours accented in red. The children were fascinated by the coloured spirals. They designed them as folding, extending shapes that could be adapted in size according to the age of the children playing with them. They could also be bent easily so that the children could shape them themselves.

technical installation. The children looked at reproductions of the Pompidou Centre, Paris, and some designs for cosmic laboratories.

The second group was formed of structures distinctly recalling natural formations. This included the spiral made of eggshells that looked like a large sea-monster capable of growing in all directions. Here we commented on architectural bionics, a science solving technical structural problems by studying and then using the clever structure of plant or animal systems, for example the structure of a stalk, a shell or a honeycomb. The architect makes

109b

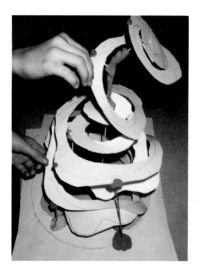

The interesting construction of a spiral; the designer tried to work out at which points it had to be supported to make it slant towards the viewer from its most interesting side.

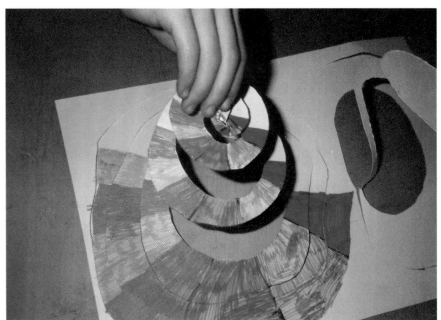

109b *This fantastic shape* is painted with cold and warm colours. The small artist worked with thick felt-tipped pens, also cutting out the shape of a small artificial pool or sandpit to go next to the shape.

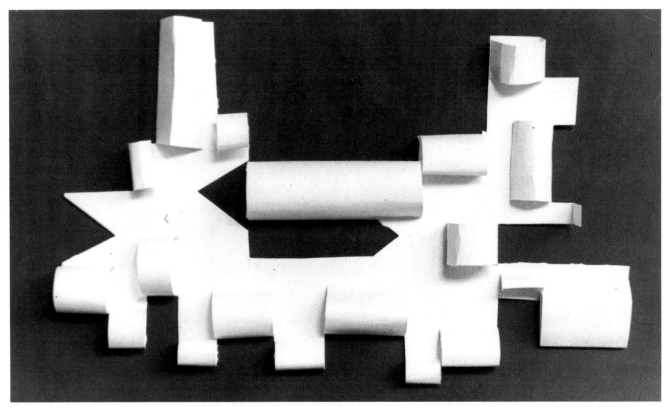

110 *Design for a decorative panel* in the hall of a railway station, but also for a set of hollow shapes for crawling and jumping through for small children in the playground. The small boy worked over the full area of a sheet of paper. He first drew stripes with a ruler (see diagram). He folded the stripes towards the centre of the paper into triangular or quadrilateral prisms, or he turned them into cylinders of varying size. In contrast to the preceding designs the vertical and horizontal articulation of the composition is preserved. Part of the folded shapes are stripes glued to the surface of the base. The whole looks like an old steam engine. Other engines could be constructed in the same way, possibly also simplified animals.

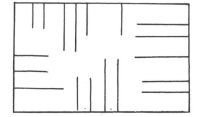

creative use of the intricate and structurally interesting models from nature. The children decided that this group also included dwellings shaped like melons and covered with aluminium foil which the author described as a self-contained house with solar panels on the roof. And so we found that there was also 'ecological architecture' whose technical installations guarantee that its functioning in no way pollutes the environment.

The third group contained models of dwellings recalling the building know-how of primitive peoples which today again inspires modern architecture. These were designs similar to Indian rock towns, tepees, clay structures in Africa and Eskimo igloos. Here belonged without doubt the structure from halved tennis and table tennis balls, partly also the 'architecture' made of polystyrene remnants and finally all the buildings that were based on the construction of various types of tents. Quite naturally these were followed by information on the recently re-introduced and created clay architecture (with a possible change to concrete), which has a functional tradition under certain living conditions and where the word 'primitive' takes on quite a new meaning. Architects are also aware that human beings living for generations in the same region had centuries to observe and verify geographical, climatic and material possibilities and thus create the most suitable forms of dwellings.

The fourth group, modern architecture of glass sky-scrapers, the architecture of 'skin and bone', included the idea of the boy who folded a long strip of soft metal into a simple high-rise skeleton. In Norbert Lynton's book *Landmarks of the World of Art: The Modern World*, the children discovered one of the 'most perfect and most austerely conceived New York business centres' – the Seagram Building erected in 1957 by the architect Ludwig Mies van der

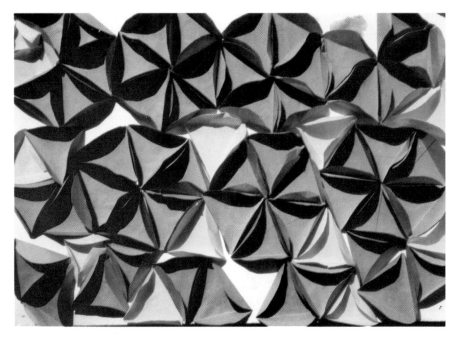

111a

111 *Older children made designs for three-dimensional walls.* They arranged simple folded paper shapes into regular rows. They glued them to a stiffer sheet of paper. Though the children used a pleasant brown gingerbread colour, this is not design for the wall of the gingerbread cottage, but to find out whether the separate elements could be made from tiles of burnt clay.

111a *The girl cut small wheels* from layers of brown and partly yellow paper which she folded three times.

Rohe and his pupil Philip Johnson. Framed glass panels are fixed to the skeleton.

The fifth group contained the children's constructions which were similar to 'poster architecture', so called because of its bright colours recalling advertising posters. The children had thought up buildings made from various boxes, all containers showing advertisements of their previous contents. The lettering was also an important decorative factor advertising the building.

If you attempt such work you will find the children untiring during discus-

111b

a   b   c

111b *Squares folded along the diagonals.* The entire surface is brightened by the inclusion of yellow triangles.

111c *A folded rectangle forms the three-dimensional surface. All variations are shown in the diagram.*

sions of their buildings. They demand commentaries on all their creations. If you have a suitable book on architecture at hand, do not hesitate to use it. Leave the children to leaf through it and try to find something similar to their designs in shape or construction in real architecture. While looking for a house similar to one of theirs, a fortress, the children were fascinated by the colour reproduction of the monumental chapel of Notre Dame du Haut at Ronchamp in eastern France, completed in 1956 by Corbusier (1887–1965). They compared it to a huge petrified ship anchored to a large lighthouse. The book also gave interesting information about children in Marseille who play on the roof of a house, where they have their playground. Corbusier concentrated flats for 3000 inhabitants (almost a small town) into one house. The 10-year-olds were terrified at the thought of having to live in such a huge house and immediately wanted to travel to Marseille to have a look at that playground. They have their own experiences of housing estates! When they looked at the reproductions of Corbusier's Villa Savoy in Poissy near Paris (1930) they longed to have a small school like that, airy and spacious and full of sunshine. And of course they imagined that their own school could be much more colourful. A small team of children decided spontaneously to draw first of all a ground plan of their subject – a complex of several interconnected flat-roofed school buildings. Then they built a small model from empty soap powder boxes glued over with white paper. This was because they wanted to decide on the colours at the very end. Wouldn't you also like to see what sort of school your

112

112 *Structure for a fair attraction.*
This interesting shape consisting of
sticks (drinking straws, spills and
metal strips) was made by adding and
arranging other material and joining it
with plasticine. The boy only later put
a coloured spiral into the construction
as a slide or track for carts.

children would design for themselves? Perhaps they will realise that fantasy
alone and free play with the model would not be sufficient for a great architect. On the other hand don't think that architects might be angry that the children make a game out of their responsible design work. Let us remember the
words we used to open this chapter. 'Man would not have built anything at all,
if children had not learned to build when playing...' Architect Jan Kaplicky, who
designs for NASA, came from Great Britain to the Czech Republic to give
a lecture. Without the slightest reservations he included among his slides of
buildings children's drawings of fantastic architectural designs.

If we study the documentation of children's work in this chapter we see
that many fantastic shapes of dwellings arose because the building material
itself dictated the technical procedure (threading, gluing, folding, making holes,
moulding, arranging side-by-side, etc). The material determined the structural
possibilities and the definitive form. A thistle behaved differently from clothes

113a *Construction of a rail track* wide enough for small wagons (a mountain or overhead cable railway). Two smaller boys were given a limited area (paper covered with polystyrene), which they had to build up with a regular and rhythmic construction. First they marked out the groundplan and then they started the construction. They used wooden spills and plasticine. This is the beginning of the work.

113a

pegs or the shells of conkers or eggshells; plastic modelling clay and plaster of Paris must be handled differently. Various types of paper present an endless variety of possibilities as shown in the children's designs for climbing frames, playgrounds and swimming pools (Pictures 107–110).

Let's try to discover what the material is capable of – essential knowledge for the contemporary builder of houses, bridges and towers. Pictures 112 to 115 demonstrate that structures of wooden sticks (spills) bring to mind

113b

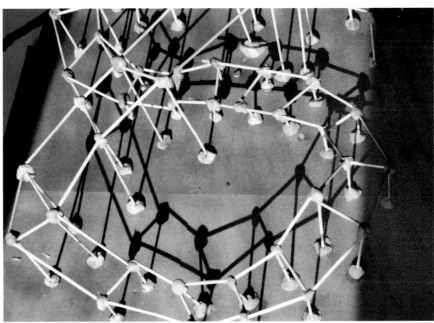

113b *Detail of a railway crossing.* Finally the boys produced a 'figure of eight'. The structure has its order. Two piers are repeated, linked with a sleeper and with small rails. Thanks to its regularity the work was easy and fast. You can also imagine how the wagons would travel along the rails.

114

metal structures. The spills here help the children to replace iron and steel. In their captions the children state that this time they imitated engineers rather than architects. We can use the opportunity to tell them about John Paxton (1803–1865), head gardener to the Duke of Devonshire, who erected a building for the Great Exhibition in London in 1851 that the admiring visitors called the Crystal Palace. It was impressive not only because of its length (about 500 metres), but also its height. A huge elm grew inside. The workmen assembled the palace from prefabricated iron, steel, cast-iron and glass parts within the unbelievably short period of nine months. Glass houses were built in the same way, as well as King's Cross Railway Station, London, by the architect Lewis Cubitt (1852). And what is so surprising about this railway station? It is erected from cast-iron ribs and two glass domes without any 'impressive' facade.

If you are now thinking of the Eiffel Tower, you are quite right. But we must remind the children that before it could be built the production of steel had to be simplified and output increased so that the French engineer Gustave Eiffel (1832–1923) could present his 300 metre high tower at the Paris Exhibition in 1889. What that meant for the World Exhibition in Prague (1892) every Prague citizen knows when he looks at Petřín Hill crowned by the small replica of the Eiffel Tower.

114 *The preceding structure photographed from the side* (113b). All good architecture is interesting from various viewpoints. Let's walk round it to choose the most interesting angle. If the structure has an order it should be easily distinguishable. The repeated upright direction will be noticeable in every side view. The rails and sleepers and the figure of eight show the order when viewed from above. The 'eight' and the movement in it has been felt by anyone who has travelled in a fast car on such a mountain track. To enable the children to see architecture 'from above' we can take them to an observation tower, a high church spire or other high structure.

115 *It is not easy to produce complete chaos.* Older girls found that out when they were given the same building material for their construction as the boys (Pictures 113 and 114). The girls laughed a lot while putting

up their 'mad' structure, although it was much more complicated. They did not know in advance how the structure would continue, they balanced the crossbeams by instinct, they tried which more daring position of the beam in space would have to be more firmly supported. Whereas the boys after having decided on the shape built the figure of eight mechanically, the girls constantly consulted with each other and quarrelled. Several times their structure collapsed and they had to think up something firmer. They were reminiscent of beetles in the grass, that must find out how to climb over stalks, twigs and needles. This construction also surprises and pleases the viewer, although it has a strange, seemingly mad, illogical arrangement of something variously balanced, supported and unevenly stressed.

How better could we finish this chapter than on the children's favourite – the construction of towers? Do you still remember what the towers were like that you built when you were a child? When small children build a tower they experience their first architectural excitement. Will it fall down? Will it stay up? It is quite a low tower, seldom higher than its small builder, usually made of building blocks, but sometimes also from damp sand. When children build their first sandcastle with one or two towers, they are usually only the helper of an older friend, sibling or a willing parent. They learn without realising it something of the strength of materials and basic building principles. They usually find that the less reliable the material, the broader the foundations must be.

Using boxes, sand, stones or pieces of wood for their structures, the small architects experience everything their ancestors did in their first building experiments. And we should let the children enjoy their creative excitement, even though they have perfectly interlocking parts of a building set amongst their toys.

Human beings erected towers as protection against enemies, they were purpose built however monumental they appeared. In Sardinia nearly 7,000 remains of 20-metre high nuraghs – defensive towers dating from the 9th to 7th century BC – have been preserved. This was not architecture as an art

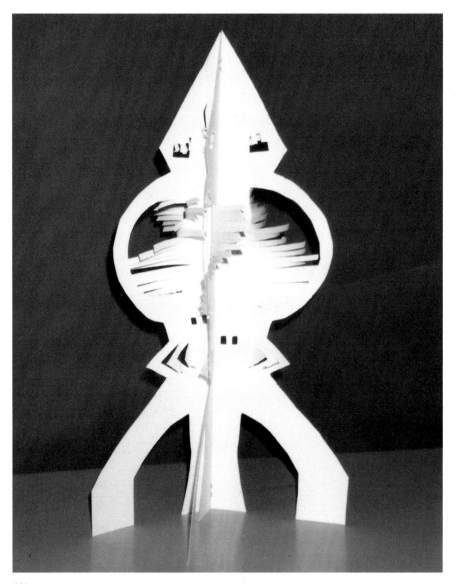

116a

116a, b *A tower or a rocket?* They have the same pointed top, get narrower towards the apex and have a firm base. Below the top all the children built a rest area for visitors to the tower, a restaurant with a view, a control centre, etc. The diagram and photograph show that the children cut two equal towers along the axis and then bent them towards each other and stapled them together.

form. Since the towers were not connected with the spiritual or religious life aesthetic criteria did not apply to them. But how can we grasp other tremendous architectural achievements such as the famous megalithic structure of Stonehenge on Salisbury Plain in the south of England from the second millennium BC? The 45 ton heavy pillars were brought from as far away as a quarry in South Wales. Did man try to test the limits of his strength and ingenuity? The tower of Babylon (Ziggurat) had a base 91 metres square and a height of 90 metres. It had seven storeys, with a temple on the top. It seems that the gods' answers to human questions on the sense of existence may only be found high up on mountains or towers. Not without reason do people recall the wise adage: 'If you want to see far, you have to grow tall.' From the temple on the top of the tower the priests observed the sky and the stars and perhaps it held good for them 'the higher the tower, the greater the understanding of the knowledge we are seeking'. Where does human ability to think and to create end? Every mathematician looks in amazement at a Gothic cathedral.

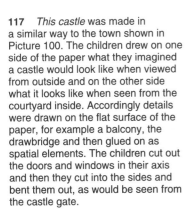

117 *This castle* was made in a similar way to the town shown in Picture 100. The children drew on one side of the paper what they imagined a castle would look like when viewed from outside and on the other side what it looks like when seen from the courtyard inside. Accordingly details were drawn on the flat surface of the paper, for example a balcony, the drawbridge and then glued on as spatial elements. The children cut out the doors and windows in their axis and then they cut into the sides and bent them out, as would be seen from the castle gate.

118

118 *Black castle*. An assemblage of bottles and abacus beads appeared in the same way as in Pictures 84a, b, c when tidying away teaching aids. It is obvious that for their fantastic spatial construction sets, children do not always require elements from expensive construction sets.

119a *The glass house* was made from a shoe box; the girl cut out the windows and doors. The entire surface is divided by two roofs in very pleasing proportions. The roofs are like those on glass houses, allowing the cultivation of tropical plants, but they could also be used as two painters' studios.

119b *This white villa* was made of several boxes of different sizes. The boy tried out various combinations before he was satisfied. Then he painted the boxes white, the roofs and window frames black. The red sphere (a bead from an abacus) is a sculpture whose round shape softens the strict lines of the building.

In northern Europe spires and arches 30 to 35 metres high reached to the sky before the year 1200. These high buildings seemed to symbolise human ingenuity and joy at having overcome the weight of stone, having resisted gravitation. But the materials set their limits. The cathedral of Rheims with a 435-metre high arch collapsed.

Baroque succeeded in breaking through the cupola from inside by the illusion of a painted sky pretending that it was transparent. So it seems that towers and spires were the extension of human thought whether in the dialogue between priests and God or astronomers and the universe. Man has given great height to modern towers welded from steel plates and anchored deep down in the earth to send and receive radio and television signals. The towers appear to exceed their dimensions – they 'leave' the earth. From the outside they recall the technically perfect rocket on the rocket base, or a minaret, a Gothic or Baroque spire (to the children they also looked like corn-on-the-cob, ragwort, foxgloves, or irises).

The towers have their roots deep within the earth like man, their tops are the symbol of the dreams and longings to recognise human possibilities. That

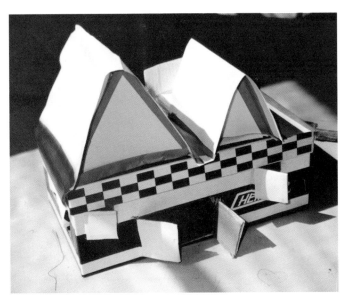

119a

119b

is why we construct models of castles or towers with the smaller children.

Prague is called the 'City of a Hundred Spires', enabling us to compare and guess from a distance whether we are looking at a Baroque or a Gothic church. You can see the new feature of the Prague skyline, the television tower, in our small art gallery.

Our considerations on architecture would not be complete if the children had not attempted a design for their own house or school. An English proverb says: 'My home is my castle'. And therefore the 10-year-old children were set the task of finding three or four shapes – these could be boxes of various sizes. They were allowed to play with them, put one on top of the other, interchange them till they were satisfied with the result. Our final illustrations show how they succeeded.

119c

119c *This school* gives the impression of a happy technical structure. The pillar supporting the upper floor is a small transparent cylinder. The girl explained that this was the outside lift to the upper storeys. The paths round the building are covered with sand which the girl scattered over the area previously painted with glue. The bushes are cut from a sponge.

A

B

C

D

A, B *Children's World Pavilon* for the Czechoslovak Jubilee Exhibition of 1991 designed by painter Stanislav Holý and built by architects Václav Lukas and František Kříž. The colours and shape were influenced by a children's construction set. This is evident from the front gate and the three decreasing blocks seen from the side. The biggest cube contained three storeys full of various games, tests and puzzles.

C The side view of the axis of the 33-m high ferris wheel in the luna park is a surprise for the spectator. When the shadows of the steel supports in the picture no longer confuse you, you see that the structure is symmetrical according to the central vertical line, thus preserving also from the side view the interesting geometrical system of the inner space.

D *Veronika Zapletalová* (born 1971), *Growing spatial structure*, 1992, coloured wooden. This asymmetrical structure was built for a large niche 4.5 m wide and 8 m high. Its size is increased by the shadows it cast. Children compare it to a mysterious crystal with only edges visible. (This is the work of a student of the Studio of spatial textile art and alternative techniques under Professor Adéla Matasová, University of Applied Arts, Prague.)

E *The television transmitter in Prague;* joint authors architects Václav Aulický, Jiří Kozák and Alex Bém, 1984–92. This brilliant piece of technical architecture towers 216 m above the surrounding area. The weight of the mast is 11,800 tonnes. Between three circular tubes, the highest of which is 6.4 m in diameter, are 'inserted three trefoils', one above the other, each containing a glass cabin. The lowest houses a café, the middle one a lookout area and the highest the technical equipment.

F *Michal Sedlák* (born 1971), *Textile fibres on a wire frame,* 1992, $350 \times 320 \times 180$ cm.
Having examined this strange tent from the inside and outside, the children conclude that this is the remains of an intelligent visitor from outer space. The four concealed black 'doors' are obviously exits to other spaces – 'black holes' in space. (The work of a student of the Studio of spatial textile art and alternative techniques under Professor A. Matasová, University of Applied Arts, Prague.)

E

F

Small people and big things. Some older children created ten plasticine puppets of equal size, as big as a large hand. The children used spills as long measuring sticks, marked the proportions of parts of the human body on them, broke them and added several more to form the 'skeleton' of the small puppet. They then modelled on the spills. The puppets' joints are as flexible as human joints. They can sit down or climb on things.

An old coffee-roaster resembles a knight or an old devil. A ten-year-old boy gave life to its 'face' with coloured chalks.

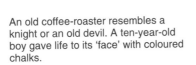

Ordinary plastic bottles can be used for ornamental sculptures. Hung up on a string they spin like windmills.

ACKNOWLEDGEMENTS
The Publishers would like to thank all
the artists for having provided the pictorial
material used in this book.